THE 9-MILE MARATHON

THE 9-MILE MARATHON
A New Breed of Marathon Runners

MARLIES KORT

The 9-Mile Marathon
A New Breed Of Marathon Runners
ISBN 978-99904-5-093-4

Revision 9.0

Published by Free and Focused Inc.
Curaçao

Printed in the United States of America

To All Marathon Runners

Living A Busy Life With Work,
Family And Friends

Dedicated to Stans van der Poel

Dutch medical researcher, for her visionary work on chronicle fatigue, recovery, cure and her contributions to the Dutch running society.

A true square peg in the round hole.

"It's easy to get wrapped up in following those 'standard' training schedules. Marlies is not just a champ, nor just a great coach. She's a visionair. Passionate about running. and sharing. Teaching. With a strong desire to exploit new insights.

Marlies teaches us how we can do without the old 'no pain no gain' mantra. It is new, and yes, disruptive. Breaking with what most coaches tell you today. Her program opened my eyes too. There isn't any other marathon training program like it. My students start to discover The 9-Mile Marathon training system now too. I have '9-Milers' in my team who ran their marathon the new way. Recently. Happy and healthy, with a strong finish. After only 9-mile (max) training runs. Even newbies. Truly remarkable."

— Dan Blankenship, Head Coach RVA Team Richmond USA

Contents

You Don't Have To Play This
Game Alone.

There are marathon runners,
including me, who want to
welcome you as a 9-Miler and
support you on your Marathon
Running journey.

Will You Join Us?

The Choice Is Yours:

www.9miler4life.com

Because The People Who Are Crazy Enough
To Think They Can Change The World, Are
The Ones Who Do

Russell Brunson

1. INTRODUCTION

November 3 2013, I won the 43rd edition of the New York City Marathon overall in the female non-professional category. It was the comeback of NYC's beloved five-borough 26.2 mile race after its previous cancellation in the wake of Superstorm Sandy. My finish time was 2h52, which was even faster than some of the participating elite pro runners who started their race right in front of me. Thanks to my 2h47 pb at Berlin the NYC organizing committee invited me to start the race at the front of the 50.000+ pack, right behind the pro's. Exciting!

In 2014 My World Fell Apart

I found myself in the middle of a divorce working my way through this process and trying to keep my twin daughters Annelot and Karlijn with me as much as possible. A complex exhausting process, not just because we wanted to play it fair to all parties involved.

May 17th, at my mother's birthday with the entire family united in my parent's house / home-ground in Zeeland The Netherlands, my father informed us that he was being diagnosed with colorectal cancer.

Additionally, in that very same year, being a professional with a degree in interior design and architecture, -due to the financial crisis at it's worst point- I had to find new ways to pay the bills. The real estate development market simply ceased to exist.

I Was Devastated

On the following pages I will tell you my story. About my desires. About the struggle, hitting the wall, juggling with the most valuable asset I had; time. Juggling with the most limited resource I had; me. Making a living, being a good mom, living my life with my two daughters, building a new company, learning, building new networks, trying to keep up and doing what I loved most at the same time:

running and triathlon. I will tell you about the breakthrough, the epiphany, the experience of my striking realization. The opportunity I discovered. Leading to where I am today. The support I received unexpectedly from this wonderful researcher. The new system it became. The transformation I experienced.

The sudden striking realization I found something new, this breakthrough, was the KEY to picking up my new life again. Today I know training The 9-Miler Way is the ONLY training system available at the market today to allow people like you and me, living a busy life with work, family and friends, finish marathons solid and strong WITHOUT the need to run those endless long and slow 18+ mile, time-consuming training runs.

So, halfway 2014, I realized I HAD to do something. I decided to start my own local fitness/ health training and personal coaching business.

In hindsight, I don't really know exactly how I survived and managed to make all ends meet. It was tough, demanding, stressful. But I knew one thing for sure though. I kept training for a next Ironman 70.3. I needed to do this. My motivator. My heartbeat. State-management. Meditation. Energizer. I felt I 'had' to do this. I'm sure you know this feeling too. Deep down I KNEW I had to. It kept me 'alive'.

Because time was very limited, I decided to do my trainings different and drastically cut the time I used to put into the long and slow training runs. I decided I was going to run shorter, and to run EVERY 'long' run at the anticipated heart rate required for the RACE.

I did this for 5-6 weeks. Feeling good. It felt like less pressure. I didn't feel tired at all. In fact, every week, I felt better. Different from what I used to experience. Because during training periods you get tired and you need to back off to recover for a couple of days (the so called 'taper' periods). But this time, training this way, it was different.

Then It Started To Happen…

I started to feel stronger. I mean stronger. WAY stronger. Like I never felt before during 'regular' marathon training prep periods. It was weird. Although I didn't train for as long and far as I used to, I started to feel stronger, fitter, empowered, with a clear mind, alert, confident. And the weirdest thing was I started to run quicker at the same heart rate! Which means with the SAME effort I became FASTER!

Later on I will explain to you EXACTLY what I did and what was happening. Because today I understand. I will also explain the SYSTEMS I implicitly developed back then to find the right heart rate and performance levels (today I call them MHR - Marathon Heart Rate definition protocol, AFA- Accumulated Fatigue Avoidance system and ESS- the initiation of the metabolic Energy Supply Switch).

Today's 9-Mile Marathon Training System is about understanding and how to implement the then 'secret' concepts of MHR, AFA and ESS.

So, while trusting this process without REALLY knowing what's was going on..

I WON at the Miami Ironman 70.3 October 2014, and by doing so, qualify for World Championship Ironman 70.3 in 2015.

And then... 9 months later, again following and trusting my new 'secret' kind of training, working my butt off at the same time building a new company, raising my 2 beautiful daughters, in the summer of 2015 in Austria..

..I BECAME WORLD CHAMPION IRONMAN 70.3 FEMALE 40-44 CLASS

One thing I knew for sure. I had reduced the number of hours on training. In a RADICAL way. Like less than 50% of the amount of time I used to. I didn't run any 'classic' long and slow training runs. They were 'banned' out of my plans! And I CHANGED THE WAY I was training. MOST of my trainings, I ran EXACTLY at race speed. I reduced the amount of bike- and swim-time -doing the same thing, i.e. skipping the long work.

And It Worked!

I created a kind of 'formula' to find these specific running/training paces. They formed the basis for the tables and formula's you're using today in The 9-Mile Marathon Training Program. This 'invention' alone meant I saved TONS of time allowing me to spend more time on the other important things of life I needed to do.

So all 'n all I trained less than 50% of the time on running I used to do, combined with an also

DRASTICALLY reduced amount of hours on swimming and biking (in fact 'cross trainings'). AND, most of my trainings, I did at the heart rate I anticipated to be racing at.

Leading to very good finish times. My run splits in the Ironman were better than ever, while my swim and bike splits remained solid.

Striking.

By the time I was about to start sharing my new secret survival training program/experiences with 'the world', I stumbled upon this article (I believe it was September 2015) about Dutch medical researcher Stans van der Poel, who had been working for 20 years on capturing and visualizing heart and lung behavior, chronicle fatigue syndrome, recovery processes from severe diseases and diabetes, and translating these principles from the medical world into training guidelines that could work for everybody. Her findings were compiled by Dutch sportswriter Koen de Jong into a book published in The Netherlands called "Marathonrevolutie" (a marathon revolution). Already that year more than 100 runners used her ideas at the Rotterdam Marathon, of which most of them were able to run with relative ease, showed very stable pacing, and generally finished in the predicted time.

After reading her book it struck me that all her findings on running and training for marathons where so similar to what I already experienced the past year. From her medical/research-based scientific background she insisted that marathon runners should never train for more than 14 kilometers (which is about 9 miles, even less than the 10 miles I trained in my 'special Marlies survival training program').

I Was So Happy To Read This!

I was so happy to find a "soul mate" who supported my ideas and experiences even with a medical background and proof from a scientific standpoint. I was immediately convinced that this researcher Stans van der Poel and I were at the same level. Stans implemented the findings from her medical research on the recovery processes of her patients, where I had to cope with the 'practical' challenges of daily life running and performing at the highest level with limited time. In essence what people like you and me all have to cope with: a busy life with work, family and friends PLUS the desire to run marathons at the big events.

Now The Big Question Was How Could This Be True?

You will find the answers in the next chapter "The Big Fat Lies About Running." It was clear that both Stans from a 'scientific' background and I coming from my 'real life' coaching, working and running background had found a 'new marathon running science'. A new running paradigm, a totally new concept. A fresh new vision on endurance running. Not complex but very simple in essence. And most of all, TOTALLY different from what the traditional coaches have told us for the past 4 decades.

In The Netherlands they called it a marathon revolution. I decided to further develop and fine-tune it from there, according to my own personal beliefs about training, living and running, taking Stans' findings into account.

I called it The 9-Mile Marathon.

And it all started from there..

I am CONVINCED this is the BEST marathon training program available on the market right now for non-elite 'age-group' runners. In this new book I will explain to you how and why, and why the 9-Mile Marathon training system is applicable to half-marathon training as well.

The 9-Mile Marathon is a blueprint for half- and full marathon training in a radical new way.

9miler4life.com

It Is Disruptive And A 'Must-Read' For Anyone Who'S Into Running

And most of all, a must-read for anyone who always wanted to run a marathon but simply can't digest those endless weekly 18+ mile training runs the 'classic' training programs and coaches tell us to do in order to be able to run a marathon.

With The 9-Mile Marathon We're Changing The Marathon Rules

Not only is it successful, it's fun -a lot more fun than the old high mileage training schedules as they are promoted by most traditional running coaches.

That may be the reason why the The 9Mile Marathon caused quite some traditional coaches' upset,

Creating Controversy And Skepticism

Mostly by running enthusiasts who are discussing and arguing but not actually testing or implementing the new program for themselves.

At the start I wondered why, but now I know. The 9-Mile Marathon is about the issues in the 'old' way of marathon running NOBODY wants to talk about. The injuries, the social stress, the fatigue, the quitting because of training overload.

Nobody's Talking About.. The Running Taboos

I'm going to arm you with insights, background information and training secrets that will help you understand why and how you can run the marathon and half marathon in a totally new way. A much better way: faster, stronger, happier *and* healthier. With less training miles. WAY less.

No Special Skills Are Required

as long as you are in good physical shape (when you are in doubt always consult your doctor first), you run for more than a year and when you're able to run 6 miles in less than like 75 minutes, we're ready to go!

Marlies Kort

Founder and Creator of The 9-Mile Marathon

More info about Marlies Kort:

In 2015 Marlies Kort became World Champion Ironman 70.3 F40-44 in Zell am See, Austria. In 2013 she won the NY Marathon 2013 non-pro female overall class. Her personal best is 2h47 Marathon Berlin. She is Female 40-44 winner of Ironman 70.3 Miami (2014), Puerto Rico (2015), Panama (2016), Cartagena (2016), Aruba (2016), Boulder (2017).

Marlies is winner and track record holder of the Aruba International Half Marathon and the KLM Curacao Marathon 2016. In Cartagena 2016 Marlies again qualified for the 2017 World Championship Ironman 70.3 F40-44 in Tennessee USA. April 2017 Marlies ran the Rotterdam International Marathon and finished 5th Overall Dutch Women including the pro's.

Marlies runs Free and Focused Inc. her life-coaching 9-Mile Marathon business based on running, dramatically changing the life of marathon runners from all over the world, who still want to run and race marathons at the 'BIG' events, living a busy life with work, family and friends. Marlies runs her business together with co-founder, her coach and partner Bastiaan Zwaan, who has a Phd from Tech University, Delft, the Netherlands. Bastiaan who is a consistent Ironman 70.3 Top-10 age-group 55-59 finisher, and, inspired by Marlies' new insights, ran his first ever marathon in 2017, 100% following The 9-Mile Marathon training program, and finished 4h07, just 2 minutes shy of the time Marlies predicted at the beginning of his 90-Day training program. Later that year he finished another marathon, the KLM Curaçao marathon, in grueling hot conditions on a hilly course, with an even more reduced training program to research the boundaries of what's possible within the 9-mile concept. With max 5-mile training runs and cross training (mountainbiking) he still managed to finish in 4h41.

Orlando Florida, March 2018

2016 Sunset training on the beach with one of my first 9-Mile Marathon coaching groups

2015 Austria WC 70.3 trail running and cross training experimenting The 9-Miler Way, resulting in becoming World Champ Ironman 70.3 F40-44 category - Half Marathon finish time 1h24

2. THE BIG FAT LIE

I have ONE question for you.

What is the biggest LIE you've been telling yourself about marathon training and running?

It is the lie about the long and slow training runs you must do in order to 'survive' your marathon, as traditional coaches told us for the past 30 years.

It is the lie about you need to suffer for 4-5 months, the old 'no pain no gain' mantra, in order to be able to make it to the starting line.

It is the lie about the need to sacrifice your personal family- and social life as soon as you pick up your marathon training program.

It is the lie you need to suffer from chronicle fatigue and injuries.

It is the lie you have to ..... (you name it)

99% of all trainers and training schedules out there tell you to run those long and slow 12-18+ miles runs in order to prepare yourself for the marathon. Long because each run will be like 2 hours or more. Slow because all trainers will tell you to run those 'long-' runs at a lower pace than your anticipated marathon race-pace. In the typical classic marathon training schedule you will be running the biggest part of your trainings at a lower pace than the pace you will be running at the big day.

Which also implicates you train most of your (precious) time at a heart rate which is too low.

In fact, the traditional programs are asking you to spend most of the time of your training at a TOTALLY different (i.e. lower) heart rate than the marathon heart rate of your race!

Think about this...

And, typically, we're looking at 40+ weekly mileage and 8-10 hour training weeks. If you are someone with a busy job, family and social life, this is hardly doable. Unless you sacrifice other important things in life. Which implicates those classic trainers are asking you to deliberately create imbalance in your life. Which creates

STRESS

And we all know stress is the number one performance killer.

Conclusion?

We have to get rid of this way of thinking. And replace it with something **NEW**.

My goal is no to FIX whats not working. My goal is to REPLACE what's not working with something COMPLETELY new.

Did you ever think of WHY 99% of today's trainers tell you the same?

Well, the answer is shocking. Hard to believe. But true.

Because they all repeat each other without ever thinking if what they're saying is true. They don't care about the truth. They just copy-paste. Repeat. What's been said for 3 decades.

Copy. Paste. Repeat. For 30 Years

Well I can tell you this. In order to successfully run marathons living a busy life with work, family and friends at the same time..

We Need Change. Real Change. We Need

NEW

With the 9-Mile Marathon training system I drastically cut training hours down. Way down— meaning you will run max 9 mile training runs, only

3 training runs per week and max 6 hours per week on training.

I hear you thinking...

Is This Possible? Could I Ever Run A Marathon With Just 9-Mile Training Runs?

The answer is YES. Definitively. Happy, healthy, stronger and faster than you'd ever expected.

But not JUST LIKE THAT. There is a smart science behind it. With a new protocol to help you finish strong, even if you ran only half the number of miles the classic schedules told you to do.

So I need your commitment. A big yes. Or a big no (in case you bail out I'm fine too; it's your choice). There is no way in between. There are no shortcuts. I want you the be a 9-Miler. Because I know t will change your life. A marathon runner living the 9-

9miler4life.com

Miler life. Balancing running, work, family and your social life with family and friends.

So... When The Answer Is A Big Yes...

Then here's the deal. What I need from you is this:

- You run for at least one year and you are able to run 6 miles in less than 75 minutes;

- You're free of injury and/or a disorder or illness that prevents you from running a full marathon (ask your doctor);

- You have a gps running watch with heart rate;

- You can commit to 90 days prep time with 3 training runs per week (max 3 to 6 hours of weekly training).

Then, in return, in order to successfully complete your marathon, your maximum long run will be just 9 miles. And you'll spend less than 6 hours per week on training and running. And, one more thing, I will

NOT ask you to train for a 4 - 6 months period! The whole prep period The 9-Miler Way is just 3 months - 90 days.

9 Miles. Yes. Just 9 Miles. And 90 Days.

To most age-group runners this is something like a 1 ¼ -1½ hour run. And you will run only 5 or 6 of those 9-mile long runs during the entire 90-Day marathon prep period.

Deal? Deal!

I mean:

DEAL!!

I've Seen So Many Runners Suffer

from those endless long and slow training runs. And I had my own fair share of injury and exhaustion as well.

I Always Felt There Had To Be A Different Way.

A NEW way of marathon training. TOTALLY NEW. That fits way better in the daily life of people like you and me, living a busy life with family, friends, work.

I translated it into a comprehensive, new, disruptive training methodology. And now I want to share it with you.

So running and training marathon CAN BE DIFFERENT. Smarter. With fewer training miles. Way less. You have to realize; this is a paradigm shift in the running society. No more bribing "I ran so and so many miles this weekend." A different ballgame. A different MARATHON training ballgame! It exists. Yes. Really.

Now, If These Words Scare You, You'd Better Stop Reading Now.

It means this book is not for you. You see, to many runners, these words bring up thoughts of the typical 'classic' running coaches. They tell you that running a marathon is only possible through those endless long and slow training runs. They will tell you have to suffer & you have to love suffer.

The truth is those established classic running coaches don't really know the latest endurance running secrets. They somehow, somewhere missed the point.

9miler4life.com

They Just Keep Saying What Everybody Said For Decades,

which is based on old beliefs.

In The 9-Mile Marathon my belief is:

"In order get yourself ready for the marathon you don't need to run those long and slow training runs. Or, to put it even stronger, my belief is that to most, the 18+ miles long runs are the No. 1 reason for failure."

Wow!

The Classic 18+ Mile Long Runs Are The Main Reason For Failure!

So if you want to succeed and boost your chances of finishing your marathon strong, happy and healthy, it is better to not run those long training runs.

>>>REPEAT:

In order to finish your marathon strong, for people like you and me (non-elite runners), it's *BETTER to* **NOT** *run those long and slow training runs.*

Still with me? Great. Then let's quickly move on.

In this book I will explain to you why this new training system is here and why it works.

The 9-Mile Marathon comprehensive -carefully balanced training system teaches you why and how you can run a marathon this new way too.

The 9-Miler Way

When you train The 9-Miler Way, chances are so much higher you will successfully complete your marathon in the finish time we defined at the beginning of your 9-Mile Marathon journey, feeling strong, healthy and energized all the way from the start to the finish line, even when it is your first one.

And then… you will be a 9-Miler too.

You join the 9-Miler 'tribe'. On the next pages you'll find what being a 9-Miler is all about.

I KNEW It Was A Lie...

So I Went On A Journey To Figure Out Why.

Follow marathon running journeys -including mine- on 9miler4life.com

3. A NEW BREED OF MARATHON RUNNERS

In the RUNNING society most people will tell you what 9-Milers are doing is IMPOSSIBLE. Yet it's happening EVERY DAY! 9-Milers are the REBELS. The 'crazy ones'. The round pegs in the square holes. They're NOT fond of the traditional running rules. 9-Milers CHANGE things. They PUSH things FORWARD. You can't ignore them. 9-Milers want to HAVING IT ALL. Living a busy LIFE with work, family and FRIENDS, AND enjoy the THRILL of running races at those BIG events. Feeling GREAT. Finish STRONG. Maybe even FASTER than they ever thought POSSIBLE.

"Because The People Who Are Crazy Enough To Think They Can Change The World, Are The Ones Who Do"

9miler4life.com

This is a quote from one of my mentors Russel Brunson actually.

So how do I know? How can I be so sure? How do I really KNOW that this new concept works?

Well, in the Netherlands, hundreds of runners ran a marathon like this. And, in the meantime, many of my running students and runners from all over the USA who downloaded my program (today we have more than 1,000 downloads) did exactly the same too.

Train Like A 9-Miler. Finish Strong. Feel Powerful. Happy. Healthy..

Most experienced runners are questioning the new method. While sitting on the fence they express their doubts. "It's not possible to run a marathon without those endless long and slow training runs." "There are no 'short cuts' to running a marathon; you MUST deliver the pain." "The 'wear and tear' of the long and slow 18+ mile training runs is needed to 'harden' yourself." "The 9-Mile Marathon must be a recipe for injury."

And they will have their questions (which I respect because they have been bombarded for 30 years with what those classic coaches have been telling us). "I don't think it will work for folks running their first marathon." Or does it? Does the program work for a marathon finish time of 4 hours? 5 hours? Or 3 hours? "I don't believe it will work for sub 4 hour marathon runners." "Does it work for experienced runners with a long running history? Can I do it all by myself or do I need coaching? And what if I really love to run those long runs? Are you telling me to quit running the long runs? Is it a shortcut? A scam?"

I Will Answer All These Questions, And More.

Today, thousands of runners adopted this new concept and ran the marathon this way, some faster than they ever did, without the burden of the classic long run-based training schedules.

9miler4life.com

With The 9-Mile Marathon training program my goal is to bring your marathon running to the next level. Or to bring you marathon running as an integrated part of the life you are living today without sacrifices to your personal, social, intellectual or professional life. I want you to experience my new insights and techniques, to be part of this new running movement, this new breed of marathon runners. Experience and share the thrill of training and running marathons The 9-Miler Way.

I Know Both Worlds

I trained my entire career the 'old fashioned' way. And I've seen SO MANY athletes suffer from the classic long run based training concept.

If one day you finish your marathon and you dedicate a small percentage of your success to what I have taught you today, I will feel like I have succeeded as well.

That's What Motivates Me

Sharing the passion of marathon running with you. Making it to the finish line. While living your life - with work, family and friends- at the same time.

As Sir Winston Churchill once said:

To each there comes in their lifetime a special moment when they are figuratively tapped on the shoulder and offered the chance to do a very special thing, unique to them and fitted to their talents. What a tragedy if that moment finds them unprepared or unqualified for that which could have been their finest hour.

This book, The 9-Mile Marathon, is your figurative tap on the shoulder. It has the ability to change your life.

The impact that the right message can have on you at the right time in your life is immeasurable. It could help to save marriages, repair families, change someone's health, grow a company and...

Run A Solid Marathon!

9miler4life.com

First of all, The 9-Mile Marathon is a

Completely New Approach To Running And Training.

The system is based on way fewer training miles. You run MAXIMUM 9 mile training runs, at marathon pace, to successfully run a marathon. At a very specific heart rate.

So what I'm saying is this. The 9-Mile Marathon is a completely new training concept for marathon running because it is based on a COMBINATION of 3 core elements:

Your MAXIMUM training run is much shorter

You run ALL your training runs at marathon pace

Your speed/pace is based on a specific heart rate

In fact, what I do with The 9-Mile Marathon is

Turning The Training World Upside Down.

Why?

Instead of telling yourself "I want to finish my marathon in …. (finish time goal)" the ESSENTIAL thing you need to do is to train at your marathon heart rate 'sweet spot', twice per week, and max 9 miles. And of course, with the help of The 9-Mile Marathon training program, FIND your marathon heart rate sweet spot MHR.

For age-group marathon runners, who want to perform well and finish their marathon in between 3 to 6 hours,

Running At M.H.R. Is The Best Guarantee To Finish Your Marathon Strong!

This way you will always get an optimized result; the best marathon you can run at THIS particular time and place.

I ALWAYS QUESTIONED the classic long 18+ mile training runs and the weekly 30+ mileage training loads for age-group runners like you and me.

Simply Because Most Age-Group Runners Get Squeezed

and worn out when the 'classic' high training load is combined with a busy life.

I also found that running FEWER training miles, exactly at the heart rate you're going to run at your marathon as well (your so called MHR),

is a MUCH more effective way to train and prepare for the big day than running those endless long training runs BELOW your anticipated marathon heart rate and pace.

In my running groups, 100% of my students who tried the system succeeded. Like Frank (49) and Caroll (38). -I changed both their names for privacy reasons.

9miler4life.com

Frank Was Going To Train For His First Marathon (New York 2016)

Frank was a good runner who did a couple of half marathons in like 1h50. His goal was sub 4 hours, like 3h45 or 3h50, which was quite ambitious for a first one.

Caroll was training for the New York marathon too. She had completed several marathons at around 5 hours.

She was very interested in my new approach

Mainly Because Of Her Busy Schedule,

which didn't allow her to do all required 'old style' 18+ miles long and slow training runs.

Most Age-Group Runners Tend To Train Too Much,

wear themselves out before they even get to the start line, get injured and wear themselves out mentally.

During the following training weeks both Frank and Caroll felt incredibly well with the new schedule. They really didn't get tired at all. They got stronger and stronger and with every training it got easier for them to maintain their running speed while staying at the same heart rate MHR.

After 5-6 Weeks They Both Started To Run Faster -At The Same Heart Rate!

And their breathing patterns slowed down too. They felt more relaxed, strong, secure, at this very same heart rate MHR.

Then, after 8 weeks (the 9-Mile Marathon training program is only 90 days, 12 training weeks and 1 final week before race-day) both Caroll and Frank were running their 6-9 mile training runs at MHR- at the required speed for their marathons!

I have to admit we did some additional things. Things that became 'standard' parts of The 9-Mile Marathon Training Program: speed/interval training - once per week- and additional core-strength training.

But MOST important:

They Felt Ready For It! They 'Knew' They Were Ready.

They felt they couldn't wait any longer.

The final training weeks were fun. Self-confident fun 7-9-mile training runs, some speed work, core- and strength training. NO fatigue at all. It was the opposite. They felt better and better towards the starting line.

Caroll finished NY in 4h52. Exactly the finish time we predicted with the new program. Very happy and healthy. With only HALF the training miles she used to do the 'classic' way in the past.

Frank Finished New York In 3H41. Extremely Fit.

Even a little bit faster than we predicted. While running the first 15 miles EXACTLY at the predicted pace and MHR, he managed to run a negative split and accelerated during the last couple of miles in the Central Park stretch. Frank too, very happy, healthy and on legs that were happy too!

Both Caroll and Frank shared the same feeling while running. The first 9 miles were gone in a blink of the eye. The half marathon mark felt like they just started. At 18 miles (double 9) they still felt incredibly well, wondering when the fatigue would 'hit'. Frank maintained that strong feeling all the way to the finish line, no weak moment. Caroll felt the fatigue creeping in only around mile 24, but still managed to finish strong.

Amazing. A truly amazing experience.

As a very experienced runner and triathlete I wanted to have some extra proof. I wanted the experience, the 'feel' myself. So after training for a couple of months the 9-Miler Way, I set a 2016 3-week challenge for myself with one half-marathon in one weekend, one full marathon (the Dutch Antilles KLM Open) and the Cartagena Ironman 70.3 qualifier for the 2017 Ironman World Championship in Tennessee.

With The 'Classic' Way Of Training This Would Have Been Impossible.

At first I felt quite uncertain because I wasn't used to train so much less miles than I used to. But it all went well beyond expectations. I ran the half-marathon 1h25. Not a pb, but close, and a solid run. In the KLM Marathon I won overall female and came in second of all men, 3h03. Finally, in the Cartagena Ironman 70.3 I won my age-group Female 40-44 and finished 6th overall including the pro ladies, running a 1h26 half marathon in grueling hot conditions.

We Couldn't Believe It.

We were all totally happy and successful with the new method.

The New 9-Mile Marathon Training Paradigm Definitively Worked.

In The 9-Mile Marathon, I will further explain to you why. And how. How YOU can successfully run a marathon or a half marathon this way too. The program is a downloadable program with the schedules, tables, formula's to find your marathon heart rate sweet spot MHR etc. It takes 90 days and 3 runs per week. Two of these runs are 6 to 9-mile training runs and one run is speedwork.

I have introduced

The Importance Of Cross- And Core Strength Training,

and good breathing. In the full training program download I will explain everything in much greater detail. At this point, The 9-Mile Marathon 'method' is primarily based on my own personal

Real Life Running And Coaching Experience.

Today I have a much deeper knowledge and understanding of this fairly complicated comprehensive system, evolving every day thanks to all feedback I am receiving from all of you marathon runners out there, how all parts work together and form an integrated, disruptive plan, the philosophy behind it with the revolutionary new running and training insights of Dutch researcher Stans van der Poel. Combined with my own running and coaching experiences of over two decades, I am grateful to be able to put it all together and publish this new groundbreaking marathon and half-marathon training program.

Marathon Runners Have A Choice Now.

The 9-Mile Marathon is a serious alternative to the 'classic' ways of endurance training, which are all based on long, slow, exhausting runs. I truly believe that for the non-elite age-group marathon runners who finish their marathon between like 3 and 6 hours, this is one of the best training programs available at the market today.

The fun part of this new approach is that

Training Is Not The Exhausting Process Anymore.

No accumulating stress or fatigue. It's the opposite! Nor is it a rigid program. The training schedule is flexible. No complex training sequences you need to follow with minute-by-minute schedules.

Everything is very basic. In 90 days the 9-Mile Program transforms you into an athlete who can run a marathon without the 'classic' physical burden of long distance running. In 90 days,

The 9-Mile Marathon Transforms You

into someone who can really enjoy running marathons, physically, emotionally, socially, intellectually, spiritually.

Compared with the schedules as they were published in the Runner's World USA January/February 2017 issue, The 9-Mile Marathon Training Program schedules reduce the required number of hours and miles by more than 60%.

This way, The 9-Mile Marathon training program allows you to

Running Marathons As Integrated Part Of Your Life,

Without Dominating It.

4. WHY DO WE RUN SO MANY MILES?

In the Runner's World January/February 2017 edition I read this training article about how to run stronger this year by contributing editor Michelle Hamilton. Her sources are Andrew Kastor, head coach of the California-based Mammoth Track Club, and Lori McGee Koch, head coach of Chicago Endurance Sports.

"When it comes to performance at any distance, your weekly volume is the most important factor," says Koch, "the more miles you log, the greater your stamina."

Reading This, I Immediately Felt Something's Wrong. I Mean Seriously Wrong.

According to Koch, to assess if they are running enough, she asks readers to compare the average weekly mileage with the following so-called 'minimum' weekly distances:

25 to 30 miles for the 5K

30 to 35 miles for the 10K

35 to 40 miles for a half-marathon

40 to 45 miles for the marathon

What? Is This 2018? Really?

Her overview is followed by a firm statement from Andrew Kastor: "If you were below, bring your volume up to these baselines." And: "If you were at or over the minimums –and not injured- a small increase might still help."

Most of the mileage should be done at an easy below-race pace. Then finally their advice is to be on the lookout for potential signs of injury.

9miler4life.com

(…)

Is this true? Do all running folks run that many miles? Is this really the 'minimum' standard for the so called 'average age-group runner completing the full marathon in, say, 4- 4 ½ hours?

I'm Afraid It Is. I'm Afraid This Is Still What They Want Us To Do And Believe.

So yes, this is what they want us to do. What they want us to believe. Today. 2018. These are well-known head coaches. This is Runner's World USA Edition, January 2017.

Same thing in the Netherlands. Dutch Runner's World Summer 2016 published a classic training schedule with weekly back-to-back slow-pace long runs of 16+ miles and 40 miles training weeks for BEGINNERS and average marathon runners.

Alarming. Yes. But Why? Where Is This Coming From?

And even worse, it looks like ALL 'traditional' coaches from nowadays are copying these standards blindly. Apparently without realizing what IMPACT this might have on the runners themselves, and the life they're living.

Because let's be honest. Do you really believe an average 38 years old -4 1/2 hours marathon runner is able to 'handle' those 45 training miles per week, the additional fitness trainings, living a busy life with family, work, friends, other hobby's, other social obligations etc. etc.?

From what I hear and experience, over 50% of all people who start to train for a marathon abandon their training because of mental, physical, emotional, hormonal, social problems.

Given The Numbers 'Traditional' Coaches Are Giving Us, I Now Understand Why.

So I decided to do a little research.

The high mileage training schedules originate from the 1970's and 1980's training schedules. All top runners ran training schedules based on long 20+ mile training runs and weekly training loads of 60-80+ miles.

Then later on in the 80's (the 'jogging' decade) the 'average' runners and joggers started to run those high mileage training runs too, trying to mimic the stars. Because what's good for them is good for me too, right?

Well, the answer is....:

NO!

No!

NO!

A bad habit, a bad way of thinking was born. Why? Because the Pro and 'Elite' athletes are simply much faster than you and me. Way much! The speed they run as their 'standard' easy training run pace is something we don't even run in our speed intervals! An elite runner who runs a marathon in like 2h30 runs a 'slow' 18 mile long run in less than 2 hours at a 'moderate 6:45min/mile pace. And that's just elite! The pro's are even faster. For a pro, an 18 mile 'slow' run on 6:45min/mile pace is like a 2 hour walk in the park.

The reality is, when YOU run a marathon in like 5 hours, your 18 mile long run will take like 3h30!

Weekly training runs of 18 miles may sound nice, but

The Reality Is That Weekly Training Runs Of 3 Hours And More Are Wearing You Out

Since the eighties, the amount of 'average' runners grew substantially. The biggest change since the 70's and 80's is the number of marathon runners.

Today many more people are running marathons and the average marathon runner is someone who runs way slower than the average runner in those days.

Which Is The Catch

Because today's coaches and their training schedules are still based on the average marathon runner of the 1980's.

A Truly Sad Conclusion About Today's Training 'Standards'

Which is: Today's training standards are NOT applicable to the 'average' runner of today. Even the established running magazines and authorities like Runner's World make the same mistake. They publish articles with advise, numbers and statements that are by no means applicable to the majority of their own readers. In reality it's even worse when you realize that most readers aren't even running marathons.

So I wanted to be sure this is true. And the truth is in the numbers right? So let's have a look at the numbers. To find out how the 'average' marathon runner evolved since 1985, I took Berlin Marathon data from 1985 and 2014:

	1985	**2014**
Number of Finishers	9,810	28,946
Finishers <3 hours	1,755(18%)	1,261(4.3%)
Finishers <4 hours	7,975(81%)	13,996 (48%)
Slowest runner	5h23'	7h18'

(Source: www.bmw-berlin-marathon.com)

Remarkable. In 2014, the number of participants almost tripled but there were fewer finishers who finished below 3 hours. In 1985, 81% of all participants finished within 4 hours. In 2014 less than half. In 2014, 15,000(!) runners finished somewhere between 4 and 7 hours.

Now here's the main result of my fact finding. Today more than 50% of all participants in the big marathons are running at a race pace of 9:10 min/ mile (5:40 min/km) and slower.

Now consider this. When race pace is like that, long training run pace is slower. When the average marathon race pace of the 'masses' is like

9miler4life.com

9:10-9:30min/mile, the average long training run pace will be slower than 10 min/mile.

Which brings us closer to the reality of today's runners. For the average age-group marathon runner (who runs the marathon at a pace of 9:10 min/mile (5:40 min/km) or slower), it takes at least 3 hours to complete the 18+ miles weekly long run, as the established coaches tell us to do.

Every weekend a long run of more than 3 hours. Which is at least ONE HOUR MORE than what the pro's are training! And during the week a minimum of 2 more 10 mile runs, which means another +1½ hour runs.

Honestly.. I Think.. This.. Is.. Crazy

Keep in mind the largest part of Runner's World Magazine readers (who aren't training for a marathon) will be even slower!

9miler4life.com

From the perspective of being a 9-Miler it really doesn't make sense anymore. With The 9-Mile Marathon Training Program you are able to run a safe and solid marathon with LESS THAN HALF the number of training miles and hours.

The Outcome Of My Research Was Quite Shocking:

1.	The classic training schedules are a 'heading for disaster' strategy to most of today's runners who have a desire to (maybe-only-once-or - just-a-couple-of-times-in-their-life) run a marathon;

2.	I found that to those who ran one or two marathons before, the classic training schedules are the main reason to not run another marathon. It is NOT the marathon itself but the 'classic' schedules coaches are asking you to commit to;

3.   The classic schedules scare-off many who are developing a first interest in marathon running (like 10k and half marathon enthusiasts);

4.   I also found that in reality, many runners who train for a marathon are skipping many of the scheduled long runs (resulting in an unbalanced preparation);

5.   In reality, many will abandon their marathon preps due to training overload, stress and/ or injury (my personal best guess: as I said before more than 50%)

According to the research of Stans van der Poel, for the average age-group athlete, it is simply NOT possible to fully recover from the amount of training load today's traditional training coaches tell us to do. The result is ACCUMULATED FATIGUE. I think this is the biggest insight Stans van der Poel gave us.

The weekly repetitive long runs are counterproductive to most of today's runners who want to run a solid marathon.

The Classic 'Taper' Periods Won't Help

Fatigue is accumulated all the way from the start of the training program and carried forward during the whole training period up until race day.

This explains the reality of today's marathon running age-group athletes: most suffer from accumulated fatigue. Many are burned out at the starting line.

Many did the full training programs 'classic coaches' told them to do >> BURNED OUT at the starting line.

Some decided to sign up for a marathon too short before race day and tried to make up their trainings-again based on using the 'classic' schedules >> again big chance they will be

Burned Out At The Starting Line

What you can see from the outside is folks standing at the starting line with pain killers due to injury, bad temper, caffeine addictions, sleeping difficulties, stomach/digestion problems, high breathing patterns (breathing difficult to control), excessively high heart rates (some even BEFORE the race starts), restlessness (often seen as 'this enthusiastic member of the running group').

My research led to QUESTIONING the 'old' training beliefs:

1. Why would those weekly slow 18+ miles training runs prepare ('harden') you for the 26-mile long run at race pace anyway? They ask you to run those endless long runs SLOWER than your race-

day pace. So there is still a huge gap between the pace you train and the pace you have to deliver on race day.

2.   Many high-mile training runs are wearing you out. Gradual, through accumulated fatigue. Bound to happen. Inevitable. Emotionally, mentally, physically and hormonal/adrenal. Later on in this book I will tell you how this 'fatigue monster' works. And why it takes WAY more time to recover than what you are told. It's a silent killer 'classic' coaches refuse to acknowledge. Why would you do/ want that?

'CLassic' Coaches Can't Tell You Either What Will Happen When You Enter 20-Mile-Plus 'No Man's Land' On Race Day

They tell you you need to run those long and slow 18+ mile training runs to 'harden' you for the final 6 miles.

BUT HOW DO THEY KNOW THIS WILL WORK?

The fact is, they don't know. The only thing they know is they BELIEVE in a strategy that THEY THINK will help you to finish your marathon.

Yet, at the same time, they ask you to commit to a running prep program that will do one thing for sure: to get you tired, injured and mentally worn out. Mind this is my PERSONAL opinion based on all age-group runners I've seen suffering from those 'classic' training schedules.

That's why I kept on searching. And probably that's why I discovered & found. And the book you're reading right now is what it became.

Waiting Will Get You Killed

Come Join Me And The Rest Of The 9-Miler Tribe

5. RUNNING SOCIETY DISRUPT

In 2016, Stans van der Poel's disruptive new visions took the Dutch running society by storm. Never had there been any sort of controversy at such a large scale before.

Many Trainers Thought -And Still Think- It's Crazy.

Many were angry.

When the dust settled there were a couple of hundreds of happy runners who ran according to her new ideas. Some of their success stories were recognized and published in the Dutch Runner's World Summer Edition 2016.

And, as I mentioned before, I also had the success stories of my own running students. With the help of

Stans' ideas I created my own models and schedules based on my personal experiences, my own training ideas and the results of my running students. Again, they were all very successful.

In The Netherlands, they called Stans method a 'marathon revolution'. They were right.

A True Running Society Disrupt

I called it differently. I wanted the name to associate with the 'core' of my belief; in order to finish your marathon strong your 'long' training run has to be only 6-9-miles at max! That's why I call it

The 9-Mile Marathon

When you start training the 9-miler way and when you finish your marathon the 9-miler way you become a 9-miler too. Many will tell you what 9-

9miler4life.com

milers are doing is impossible. They will even want to CONVINCE you it's not possible. But the reality is it's happening every day. 9-milers are the REBELS of the running society. The 'crazy ones'. They push things FORWARD. In a COMPLETELY new way. Doing away with the old beliefs the classic coaches and media keep telling you today. Which is always hard to accept. The choice is up to you.

Are You Willing To Become That Round Peg In The Square Hole?

When you do please continue. When you don't, better stop reading here. Final warning! This is your last chance to quit.

6. MHR, AFA AND ESS

3 key components are the basis of the philosophy behind The 9-Mile Marathon concept:

1-Marathon Heart Rate 'sweetspot' (MHR)

2- Accumulated Fatigue Avoidance (AFA)

3- Energy Supply Switch (ESS)

MHR is the personal Marathon Heart Rate 'sweetspot' we determine with a specific 9-Miler test protocol and a 9-Miler system related formula. Every runner has his own, personal MHR he/she not only uses during the race but also during ALL 9-Miler 'long' runs.

AFA

Most age group athletes train too much and too long. They simply follow the schedules they get from today's magazines, online coaches and web pages. All based on the 'classic' assumption that running more miles makes you better. Always, as a general principle. You always think you have to train more.

But during my difficult years in 2014 and 2015, I started to question this and thanks to the findings of Stans van der Poel I completely did away with it. I have started to think in a totally different way. And now I am convinced it's different. It is the opposite actually. The suggested training miles are too much. Way too much.

Too many miles for average runners leading to unwanted fatigue accumulation halfway the training progress. Causing all kinds of trouble. The 9-Mile Marathon way is designed to completely stay clear of any kind of fatigue accumulation. The 9-Mile Marathon assumes that –in order to optimally prepare you for race day- it is more beneficial for you to not accumulate any form of fatigue than the benefits of having a couple of those 18+miles slow training runs under your belt.

A new balance. In the 9-Mile Marathon Training Program we call it the concept of Accumulated Fatigue AVOIDANCE.

ESS

Carbohydrates (carbs) storage in your body allows for a maximum of 2 hours of energy. Fats stored in your body allow you to keep going for days. The 9-Mile Marathon way is designed to train your body to become more efficient in generating a higher percentage of energy from fats instead of carbs. Right from the start up until the finish. The 9-Mile Marathon way will train your body to start burning fats quicker and in a higher percentage. That's what we call the metabolic energy supply switch ESS. Once this process has started to take place it will continue and will be further developed and fine-tuned. It will turn your body into a lean and mean endurance machine, performing on endurance at the same level or better, with hardly any craving for sugar.

The 9-Mile Marathon way assumes that endurance performance will always benefit from making the metabolic energy supply switch ESS; from being a sugar burner to becoming a natural fat burner.

I am convinced that every healthy person can make this energy supply switch and complete the full distance marathon at a realistic performance level in a balanced and healthy way.

7. ACCUMULATED FATIGUE AVOIDANCE (AFA)

I am not afraid to state that in many cases the long runs and 40+ miles per week training schedules are the actual reason why most age group athletes get into trouble and quit their marathon running preps. The effect of those long training runs is the opposite of what the classic running coaches make you believe. The long runs aren't preparing and 'hardening' you for race day. On the contrary, I believe they are the number one reason for failure.

I'll tell you why. Because the accumulation of fatigue is a silent killer. Like boiling the frog slowly.

There are 2 types of fatigue that will creep in slowly:

Mental/hormonal fatigue and physical fatigue.

Mental/hormonal fatigue accumulation can be purely mental (like stress from work) and hormonal (hormone and neurotransmitter level fluctuations). These processes are the main reason why runners lose their enthusiasm and motivation during the 'classic' 18+ mile training schedules. You start doubting yourself: "Why do I want this?"or "Why do I do this?". Many will start to fear the thought of running a marathon, the suffering and the sacrifice it will require. "When these long runs already ask so much of me, what will the full distance be like?" I don't think I want that. I don't think I can do this. Combined with the overly long 'classic' training periods (4 months and more) and the accumulation of lots of training miles, it is very likely that this type of fatigue will knock on your door.

Hormonal/adrenal fatigue is a response to the stress of those overly-long training runs. The stress generated by those long runs can bring on big hormonal/adrenal fluctuations and sudden rises of insulin production which cause the blood sugar to drop too much, causing additional feelings of exhaustion.

When runners start to drink coffee way more than they are used to, it tells me that they possibly suffer from this type of fatigue. My guess is that 50% of those who quit during their prep weeks suffer from hormone/adrenal levels fluctuations, which cause mental fatigue, leading to less motivation or even pulling out of the training altogether.

The second type of fatigue that will slowly creep in is physical fatigue. Physical -running related- fatigue is caused by

1- limited oxygen supply (breath), 2- limited energy storage in muscle tissue and 3- overload related injuries in joints and filaments.

Re. 1- Recovery from fatigue caused by limited oxygen supply is quick. After a sprint your breath is stabilized within 2 or 3 minutes.

Re. 2- After a long training or a race the sugar storage in your muscle cells needs 1 or 2 days to get back to normal levels.

9miler4life.com

Re. 3- Repair of micro-injuries in joints and filaments caused by heavy training, long runs or races, need 2-3 weeks (!) to fully recover. Micro-injury related recovery from a marathon may even take 5-6 weeks.

The last type of physical accumulated fatigue, in particular, is the main reason why it is so frustrating for most runners as the weekly long runs get longer and longer. For most, the first 15-18 miles long run will be fine. In a week's time, the energy storage in the muscle tissue will be back to normal levels. But the micro-injuries in joints and filaments are not fully recovered yet. So the second or third long run will still be ok but less smooth. You start wondering why the first long run went so smooth, while the second and third long runs feel 'different'. By the time the classic training schedule tells you to do your fourth and fifth 18+ mile long run, you may be ready to decide to skip this one. You feel it's really better to stay home because for some reason you feel you're not up to it- you're tired, or worse, you feel that shady little injury somewhere scratching the surface.

The 9-Mile Marathon is designed to not get you there. No build-up of any sort of fatigue. No physical accumulated fatigue, no mental-, hormonal- or adrenal- based accumulated fatigue.

In particular, The 9-Mile Marathon training philosophy will show you that:

1- High mileage, high load training programs extending 100 days with 18+ miles training runs and 30+ miles per week training volumes are not the right basis for age-group runners like you and me to successfully prepare for a marathon;

2- In order to prepare yourself for a marathon, it's more efficient and sufficient to frequently train medium-long 5-9 mile runs at marathon heart rate, than to weekly run high mileage, high wear-and tear, long and slow training runs;

3- You won't find any 'taper' weeks in The 9-Mile Marathon training schedule. Taper weeks are designed by classic coaches to recover from too much training in the weeks before the race. The 9-Mile Marathon doesn't want you to build any fatigue at all. No need to taper during your 90 days preparations; we're only holding back in the week right before the race.

8. ENERGY SUPPLY SWITCH (ESS)

In our modern, Western society, we have trained our bodies to be eager to use carbs for energy. But carbs can only be stored in limited quantities (glycogen). "We think of carbs as the [nutrient] that's used first," says Eric Westman, MD, MHS, director of the Lifestyle Medicine Clinic at Duke University Medical Center. "We can only store a day or two of glycogen. After a quick stop in the liver, glucose enters the circulatory system, causing blood glucose levels to rise. With the help of insulin the body's (muscle) cells gobble up this mealtime bounty of glucose and store it in the form of glycogen." (www.dukehealth.org)

Once the cells have had their fill of glucose as glycogen, the liver stores some of the excess. This is a survival process. The liver serves as glycogen storage, for distribution between meals, should blood glucose levels fall below a certain threshold.

All in all the body can store about 500 grams of glycogen (which delivers about 2000 calories) in the liver and muscle cells. A marathon requires 3500 calories on average. It is easy to see why you can't run the full marathon on your carbs storage.

When you are running, your maximum carbs intake and processing capacity is 30-40 grams per hour. Each gram of carbs delivers 4 calories. A five-hour marathon means maximum 600-800 calories intake. Together with the stored 2000 the total sum of 2600 calories is by no means sufficient to complete your marathon.

So now what?

Let's have a look at the second foundation of The 9-Mile Marathon: the metabolic Energy Supply Switch.

If there is leftover glucose beyond what the liver can hold, it will be turned into fat for long-term storage, so none is wasted. For the 'regular,' Western-society-adapted-body only the scarcity of   carbs triggers the body to start burning fats. The body will be triggered to run on fat only when carbs are scarce, which is hardly ever the case. The natural survival mode. If the energy needs exceed those provided by the calories in the diet and the glucose storage in the body, the body must liquidate some of its fat tissue for energy.

The fact is, we have used our bodies too much to make use of the ever-available carbs, because there is always such an abundance of those quick and easy carbs. We have 'spoiled' our bodies and transformed them into carbs-addicted systems. The good news is the body knows how to burn carbs and knows how to burn fats too. Research by Stans van der Poel (a.o.) shows that the body is clever enough to turn back to burning fats again.

The aim of The 9-Mile Marathon program is to transform the muscles in such a way that they are taught and trained to get a higher percentage of energy from burning fats. Fats stored in the muscle cells (for immediate use), and fats released from fats storage and delivered to the muscle cells, as a fill-up. Our goal is to initiate and optimize this process and have the muscle cells change from "glycogen first" to "glycogen and fat right from the start." The result will be that glycogens are burned at a much slower rate (percentage-wise).

The 9-Mile Marathon training program is designed to help your body make this metabolic energy supply switch. And most important, The 9-Mile Marathon is designed to make the switch and optimize the process exactly at race pace.

This is a huge difference from the classic endurance training programs. They all have one thing in common: they let you run your long runs at a lower pace than your race pace. In The 9-Mile Marathon, the long run heart rate is the same as your marathon race pace heart rate. Why would you train your body's metabolic program hour-after-hour, mile-after-mile at a lower heart rate than the heart rate you will have on race day? I am convinced this is the reason why most runners who trained those endless long and slow training miles still get to know the 'man with the hammer' on race day! Although you did those huge numbers of training miles, your body is still not trained well enough to perform at your specific race pace on race day. Your body will have adapted and maybe even have made the required metabolic switches, but not at the right levels!

In The 9-Mile Marathon I emphasize running at the very same heart rate on both race day and during your endurance training sessions.

This is at a personal heart rate we call MHR – Marathon Heart Rate.

I have always been a fan of interval training. An example of interval based training is what we learned in the Netherlands from Verheul. The 'Verheul method' was based on lots of full-recovery interval and speedwork below threshold, lots of rest and medium-length endurance training with lots of variations and playful elements (fartlek). Back in those days Verheul already promoted cross training and strength. Verheul didn't promote endurance training at all. The only moment to really dig deep (in both intensity and length) was, according to Verheul, on race day.

I found the same vision applies to The 9-Mile Marathon. No slow long runs at all and if you add regular, full-recovery interval training (which is by definition at a higher intensity) the metabolic energy supply switch process is accelerated even more. It is a combination of medium-length endurance at race pace together with full-recovery intervals and speed work. That's why you will find that The 9-Mile Marathon emphasizes regular interval training and speed training with higher output levels (still below anabolic threshold).

It seems the body can be taught to optimize this process and to become extremely efficient with the fat burning cycle. As a result, you will be able to run faster, with the same perceived effort at the same heart rate. It is like Western running society habits reverse engineering. Endurance athletes, like us runners, suddenly have a far greater capacity for creating energy, without the reserves becoming exhausted too quickly (as they do with carbs).

The metabolic energy supply switch will happen in a couple of weeks' time after you have started with the 90-Day program. It means that after a couple of weeks you will start noticing it takes less effort (read: lower heart rates) to maintain the same speed. Or, you may find yourself running faster at the same heart rate.

Most runners of today who are training the classic way behave like someone with a burnout. People with burnouts or other stress- related diseases always feel tired burning sugar at an insane rate. The opposite of what we want with The 9-Mile Marathon. People with a burnout even burn sugar when they are sitting quiet. Their minds are restless and their breathing is quick and high. In the research Stans van der Poel did on chronic fatigue syndrome, diabetes and weight problems, she practiced a simple remedy: breathing techniques and easy exercise like running.

Her main conclusion was that through better breathing and aerobic exercise the 100% sugar-burning process was reversible. With chronic fatigue syndrome patients,   she managed to reverse the process and teach the body to start using fats again as a source of energy. Slowly, step by step. Through running and exercise at a very specific heart rate.

A balanced body means the energy supply program works in such a way that there is an abundance of energy available during the entire length of the day. A balanced athletes body means the energy supply program works in such a way that there is an abundance of energy available during the entire length of the run. The 9-Mile Marathon teaches the body to optimally perform at marathon-pace level and use fats as a primary source right from the first step you take.

Stans van der Poel went on and she found that this new state of balance is achieved best and quickest with frequent medium-long runs at a very specific heart rate. In The 9-Mile Marathon program we call this MHR. A bit higher than the classic long run heart rate, but way below anaerobic threshold. The optimum length of those specific runs -- 70-80 minutes or around 9 miles (14 km) for most of us -- serves to initiate and further maintain the metabolic switch ESS, without causing any accumulation of fatigue.

In The 9-Mile Marathon we train our bodies to become more efficient in generating a higher percentage of energy from fats instead of carbs. As a result your body will start burning more fats quicker and at a higher percentage.

For example, at a heart rate of 150 bpm, today you would run a pace of 9 min/mile, while 75% of your energy supply would be generated from burning glycogen, and 25% from burning fats.

After you completed the The 9-Mile Marathon 90-Day training program, once your body makes the metabolic ESS , it is very likely you will be able to run the same pace at a heartrate of f.i. 140, and a higher percentage of your energy, like 40%, will be generated from fats and 60% from sugars. This is a huge transformation which is very likely to help you to get through the difficult final stages of your marathon.

Even more so, when you look at the ultra runners society, the numbers and percentages are way more in favor of the fat burning rates. Ultra runners have transformed their bodies in extreme ways to burn fats. They can go on for days. When you look at the number of hours these people are able to keep on going at even moderate levels of intensity, they must have enabled themselves to use fats as their main source of energy, while only using sugars for other vital body functions -such as the brain- and when they have to deliver extra power like during climbs etc.

It may seem like magic, but in fact, it has more to do with science. And a new mindset, a new way of thinking. A revolution, maybe. Running and training

The 9-Mile Marathon way. Disrupting the running society.

9. CHR TEST

Now here's something really new.

You will run ALL of your 'long' training runs AND your marathon (the 'race') at the SAME heart rate: Your Personal Marathon Heart Rate (MHR). This means that, in The 9-Mile Marathon training program, you will no longer run those long and SLOW training runs from the classic training programs. And no more running at a higher pace on race day than what you are used to.

No More Slow Training Runs

MHR is COMPLETELY personal. In order to be able to calculate your MHR we will first find your Critical Heart Rate (CHR).

It is easy to find your CHR with the following test. For this test you will need to bring your GPS watch with the heart rate monitor. Make sure you display speed (km/h), heart rate (bpm) and time.

You could use min/mile or min/km, but, with the km/h the test is WAY easier. Because the test increases every 2 minutes with 1 km, which is an easy read. The "plus-1km/h-per-2-minutes" steps translate to min/mile or min/km pace steps which are way more difficult to read while doing the test. I therefore strongly advise you to configure your display on speed in km/h, heart rate and time, just for the sake of this test!

For an accurate test you need to find a flat 1 mile stretch without too much wind.

Start to run (really VERY very slow!), like dribbling, for 15 minutes at 7km/h (13:47 min/mile). After this you're ready to start with the test.
Which basically means: speeding up with +1 km/h every 2 minutes:

9miler4life.com

Minute 1 and 2: 8 km/h=12:04 m/mile=7:30 m/km

Minute 3 and 4: 9 km/h=10:44 min/mile=6:40 m/km

Minute 5 and 6: 10km/h=09:39 min/mile=6:00 m/km

Minute 7 and 8: 11km/h=08:46 min/mile=5:27m/km

Minute 9 and 10: 12km/h=08:03 min/mile=5:00m/km

Minute 11 and 12: 13km/h=07:26 min/mile=4:37m/km

Minute 13 and 14: 14km/h=06:54 min/mile=4:17m/km

Minute 15 and 16: 15km/h=06:26 min/mile=4:00m/km

Minute 17 and 18: 16km/h=06:02 min/mile=3:45m/km

Minute 19 and 20: 17km/h=05:41 min/mile=3:32m/km

Minute 21 and 22: 18km/h=05:22 min/mile=3:20m/km

Minute 23 and 24: 19km/h=05:05 min/mile=3:09m/km

Minute 25 and 26: 20km/h=04:50 min/mile=3:00m/km

So, when you do the test, you keep accelerating every 2 minutes with +1km/h until you think you have reached your maximum speed. Once you're at your max speed, maintain this speed and keep pushing hard. You keep on going, keep on pushing for as long as you can. Don't slow down! Keep up that speed! Maintain this speed for as long as you can, which is 2 minutes at max.

Then, right after you give up, you read your final max- heart rate and remember it, together with the final max- speed you reached at that moment.

So, the max speed you need to remember is the speed you reached in your final 2 minutes stretch, which you couldn't complete apparently. When you have to abort while running 16 km/h, the speed you remember is 16 km/h.

The heart rate you're reading right after you have to quit doesn't last long so you have to be quick reading it. I mean really quick because your heart rate will drop at least 5 bpm after less than 10s.

This heart rate is NOT your Critical Heart Rate CHR YET. To calculate your CHR we have to make small corrections, based on the max speed you reached. This is how you do this:

Max speed up to 11km/h: Final heart rate reading plus 6

Max speed 12-13km/h: Final heart rate reading plus 3

Max speed 14-15km/h: Final heart rate reading no correction

Max speed 16-17km/h: Final heart rate reading minus 3

Max speed 18-19km/h: Final heart rate reading minus 6

Max speed 20+km/h: You're probably too fast for The 9-Mile Marathon training system!

Example 1. You reached max 13km/h. Your heart rate is 172 bpm after you kept on pushing for as long as you could while running 13km/h. Then your CHR is 172 + 3 = 175 bpm.

Example 2. You reached max 18km/h. Your heart rate is 162 bpm after you kept on pushing for as long as you could while running 18km/h. Then your CHR is 162 - 6 = 156 bpm.

Example 3. You reached 11km/h. Your heart rate is 183 bpm after you kept on pushing for as long as you could while running 11km/h. Then your CHR is 183 + 6 = 189.

Example 4. You reached 15km/h. Your heart rate was 158 after you kept on pushing for as long as you could while running 15km/h. Then your CHR is 158 bpm.

Now You Have Found Your Critical Heart Rate!

We will use this CHR to determine your Marathon Heart Rate, your personal MHR, the cornerstone of The 9-Mile Marathon program.

Why do we make these plus 3, minus-3, minus-6 etc. corrections? Well, I found that the somewhat slower runners have more difficulty to really push themselves to the max. Most of the somewhat slower runners tend to quit their effort a bit early. Not because they want, but simply because their bodies aren't used to really pushing themselves to the max. Most of these "slower" runners do not do speedwork or interval training either. For this reason they are not used to pushing themselves in the higher heart rate zones.

Speedwork And Interval Training Is An Essential Part Of The 9-Mile Marathon Training Program,

with just ONE goal: to train your body to adapt and to perform at different levels of performance, and to create 'resistance' for the final miles of the race. Most somewhat slower runners don't like speedwork. In The 9-Mile Marathon online downloadable

Training Program you'll find speedwork and interval trainings I have designed particularly for 9-Milers.

On the contrary, very fast and highly trained runners are used to running very close to their max. They have a huge (mental and physical) resistance. They can easily run above their CHR for an extended time. The faster you get as a runner on the shorter distances like 5 and 10K, the better you are able to dig deep. We mean really deep. That's why we have to 'protect' the faster runners a bit against themselves with slightly lower heart rates for when they are going to train the long distances.

10. MARATHON HEART RATE (MHR)

Ok. So you will run ALL of your long training runs at this particular heart rate, the MHR, Marathon Heart Rate. And you will run at this very personal MHR on race day as well.

The MHR you determine today will be the MHR you use for the next 90-Day training period AND the race.

This is EXTREMELY IMPORTANT. So let me repeat:

The MHR you determine today will be the MHR you use for the next 90-Day training period AND the race.

If you are going to do another marathon later on, I advise you to do the CHR test again which will result in a different MHR probably.

Your MHR is based on your CHR and the fastest 10k run you did in the past 12 months. When you know your fastest 10k in #minutes, it is easy to find your MHR with the following equation:

MHR = CHR - 10k time (in minutes) + 28

When you know your best 10k time, and your CHR, you can also use the tables you'll find later on in the book. You just have to look for the table with the 10k time you ran and find the CHR you tested. Right next to the CHR you then found you will find your MHR.

Below you will find a couple of sample calculations.

Example 1. Your CHR is 175. You run 10k in 58 minutes. Your MHR is 145 bpm.

Example 2. Your CHR is 156. You run 10k in 39 minutes. Your MHR is 145 bpm.

Example 3. Your CHR is 189. You run 10k in 62 minutes. Your MHR is 155 bpm.

Example 4. Your CHR is 158. You run 10k in 52 minutes. Your MHR is 134.

In The 9-Mile Marathon training program you run each and every long run using your personal MHR.

The MHR is not a fixed number. It is a zone. In the beginning of the 90-Day training period, some will feel like you have to constantly push yourself to get to your MHR. Others will have to control their running speed in order to stay at the calculated MHR. In every case please feel free to use a margin around the fixed number of a couple of beats, like +/-3bpm.

Use A Margin Of +/-3 Bpm While Running

When your MHR is calculated at 140 bpm f.i., and you feel you have to constantly push to get there, it is safe to stay at the low side, like 138 bpm, on average, of your 6-9 mile long run.

And vice versa.

When you feel like you have to hold back all the time you can safely add 2 or 3 heartbeats. In that case, when your MHR is calculated at 140 bpm, it is ok to stay at the high side and run at 142 bpm on average of your 6-9 mile long run.

If you have the ambition to run a marathon while your 10k finish time is close to- or more than 75 minutes, I advise you to first train to run your 10k a bit faster. Why? Well, consider this. When running a 10k takes more than 75 minutes it will probably mean your marathon will take over 6 hours. Which is beyond the scope of The 9-Mile Marathon training program. Once you can run your 10k within 75 minutes it is safe to apply for The 9-Mile Marathon training program and use the schedules to prepare

9miler4life.com

yourself for the marathon. And finish well within 6 hours.

With most of my students the running speed at the calculated MHR is initially perceived a bit slow. Most are used to pushing harder. So you have to trust and be patient. To some this may be difficult. Mentally. In particular, in the beginning weeks, you have to stay strong to keep believing this will work, keep running at your MHR and not be persuaded by your inner voice (or your running peers) telling you to go faster.

Do Not Crack Under Peer Pressure!

Your MHR Speed will gradually increase during the 90-Day prep period. Your body will get used to this type of training. Allow it to take some time. So far, with the runners we have trained, the big 'switch' happens somewhere between 4 and 6 weeks. By then everything seems to 'loosen' up, get easier, lighter. And, without really pushing, your speed -at the same heart rate- will increase, up to the speed you find specified in the tables.

For most of my running students, in the final weeks of preparation, running 9 miles at MHR is completely effortless.

When you reach this state your body has transformed and completed the metabolic energy supply switch. You feel as if you can keep on going forever.

And This Is Exactly What I Wanted You To Experience!

It is a great feeling. The only challenge for you then is to keep holding back and wait for 'the big day'!

You can calculate your personal MHR with the above formula, the CHR that came out of your test and your 10k time in minutes.

9miler4life.com

And, as I said earlier on, another way to find your MHR is to use the tables on the following pages. The tables are sorted at your 10k time in minutes. So you have to find the table with the 10k time that matches yours. Then find your CHR (the heart rate you determined in your CHR test) and you will find your personal MHR right next to your CHR.

Your MHR is your Marathon Heart Rate 'Sweet Spot'.

Your MHR will get you anywhere!

Your 10k time is 35 minutes. You did the CHR test. You will find your personal MHR right next to your CHR:

Your 10k time is			
35			
CHR	MHR	CHR	MHR
140	133	170	163
141	134	171	164
142	135	172	165
143	136	173	166
144	137	174	167
145	138	175	168
146	139	176	169
147	140	177	170
148	141	178	171
149	142	179	172
150	143	180	173
151	144	181	174
152	145	182	175
153	146	183	176
154	147	184	177
155	148	185	178
156	149	186	179
157	150	187	180
158	151	188	181
159	152	189	182
160	153	190	183
161	154	191	184
162	155	192	185
163	156	193	186
164	157	194	187
165	158	195	188
166	159	196	189
167	160	197	190
168	161	198	191
169	162	199	192

Your 10k time is 36 minutes. You did the CHR test. You will find your personal MHR right next to your CHR:

Your 10k time is				
36				
CHR	MHR		CHR	MHR
140	132		170	162
141	133		171	163
142	134		172	164
143	135		173	165
144	136		174	166
145	137		175	167
146	138		176	168
147	139		177	169
148	140		178	170
149	141		179	171
150	142		180	172
151	143		181	173
152	144		182	174
153	145		183	175
154	146		184	176
155	147		185	177
156	148		186	178
157	149		187	179
158	150		188	180
159	151		189	181
160	152		190	182
161	153		191	183
162	154		192	184
163	155		193	185
164	156		194	186
165	157		195	187
166	158		196	188
167	159		197	189
168	160		198	190
169	161		199	191

Your 10k time is 37 minutes. You did the CHR test. You will find your personal MHR right next to your CHR:

Your 10k time is 37			
CHR	MHR	CHR	MHR
140	131	170	161
141	132	171	162
142	133	172	163
143	134	173	164
144	135	174	165
145	136	175	166
146	137	176	167
147	138	177	168
148	139	178	169
149	140	179	170
150	141	180	171
151	142	181	172
152	143	182	173
153	144	183	174
154	145	184	175
155	146	185	176
156	147	186	177
157	148	187	178
158	149	188	179
159	150	189	180
160	151	190	181
161	152	191	182
162	153	192	183
163	154	193	184
164	155	194	185
165	156	195	186
166	157	196	187
167	158	197	188
168	159	198	189
169	160	199	190

Your 10k time is 38 minutes. You did the CHR test. You will find your personal MHR right next to your CHR:

| | Your 10k time is | | | |
| | 38 | | | |
CHR	MHR		CHR	MHR
140	130		170	160
141	131		171	161
142	132		172	162
143	133		173	163
144	134		174	164
145	135		175	165
146	136		176	166
147	137		177	167
148	138		178	168
149	139		179	169
150	140		180	170
151	141		181	171
152	142		182	172
153	143		183	173
154	144		184	174
155	145		185	175
156	146		186	176
157	147		187	177
158	148		188	178
159	149		189	179
160	150		190	180
161	151		191	181
162	152		192	182
163	153		193	183
164	154		194	184
165	155		195	185
166	156		196	186
167	157		197	187
168	158		198	188
169	159		199	189

Your 10k time is 39 minutes. You did the CHR test. You will find your personal MHR right next to your CHR:

Your 10k time is			
39			
CHR	MHR	CHR	MHR
140	129	170	159
141	130	171	160
142	131	172	161
143	132	173	162
144	133	174	163
145	134	175	164
146	135	176	165
147	136	177	166
148	137	178	167
149	138	179	168
150	139	180	169
151	140	181	170
152	141	182	171
153	142	183	172
154	143	184	173
155	144	185	174
156	145	186	175
157	146	187	176
158	147	188	177
159	148	189	178
160	149	190	179
161	150	191	180
162	151	192	181
163	152	193	182
164	153	194	183
165	154	195	184
166	155	196	185
167	156	197	186
168	157	198	187
169	158	199	188

Your 10k time is 40 minutes. You did the CHR test. You will find your personal MHR right next to your CHR:

CHR	MHR		CHR	MHR
		Your 10k time is **40**		
140	128		170	158
141	129		171	159
142	130		172	160
143	131		173	161
144	132		174	162
145	133		175	163
146	134		176	164
147	135		177	165
148	136		178	166
149	137		179	167
150	138		180	168
151	139		181	169
152	140		182	170
153	141		183	171
154	142		184	172
155	143		185	173
156	144		186	174
157	145		187	175
158	146		188	176
159	147		189	177
160	148		190	178
161	149		191	179
162	150		192	180
163	151		193	181
164	152		194	182
165	153		195	183
166	154		196	184
167	155		197	185
168	156		198	186
169	157		199	187

Your 10k time is 41 minutes. You did the CHR test. You will find your personal MHR right next to your CHR:

Your 10k time is 41			
CHR	MHR	CHR	MHR
140	127	170	157
141	128	171	158
142	129	172	159
143	130	173	160
144	131	174	161
145	132	175	162
146	133	176	163
147	134	177	164
148	135	178	165
149	136	179	166
150	137	180	167
151	138	181	168
152	139	182	169
153	140	183	170
154	141	184	171
155	142	185	172
156	143	186	173
157	144	187	174
158	145	188	175
159	146	189	176
160	147	190	177
161	148	191	178
162	149	192	179
163	150	193	180
164	151	194	181
165	152	195	182
166	153	196	183
167	154	197	184
168	155	198	185
169	156	199	186

Your 10k time is 42 minutes. You did the CHR test. You will find your personal MHR right next to your CHR:

| | Your 10k time is | | |
| | 42 | | |
CHR	MHR	CHR	MHR
140	126	170	156
141	127	171	157
142	128	172	158
143	129	173	159
144	130	174	160
145	131	175	161
146	132	176	162
147	133	177	163
148	134	178	164
149	135	179	165
150	136	180	166
151	137	181	167
152	138	182	168
153	139	183	169
154	140	184	170
155	141	185	171
156	142	186	172
157	143	187	173
158	144	188	174
159	145	189	175
160	146	190	176
161	147	191	177
162	148	192	178
163	149	193	179
164	150	194	180
165	151	195	181
166	152	196	182
167	153	197	183
168	154	198	184
169	155	199	185

Your 10k time is 43 minutes. You did the CHR test. You will find your personal MHR right next to your CHR:

Your 10k time is 43			
CHR	MHR	CHR	MHR
140	125	170	155
141	126	171	156
142	127	172	157
143	128	173	158
144	129	174	159
145	130	175	160
146	131	176	161
147	132	177	162
148	133	178	163
149	134	179	164
150	135	180	165
151	136	181	166
152	137	182	167
153	138	183	168
154	139	184	169
155	140	185	170
156	141	186	171
157	142	187	172
158	143	188	173
159	144	189	174
160	145	190	175
161	146	191	176
162	147	192	177
163	148	193	178
164	149	194	179
165	150	195	180
166	151	196	181
167	152	197	182
168	153	198	183
169	154	199	184

Your 10k time is 44 minutes. You did the CHR test. You will find your personal MHR right next to your CHR:

Your 10k time is			
44			
CHR	MHR	CHR	MHR
140	124	170	154
141	125	171	155
142	126	172	156
143	127	173	157
144	128	174	158
145	129	175	159
146	130	176	160
147	131	177	161
148	132	178	162
149	133	179	163
150	134	180	164
151	135	181	165
152	136	182	166
153	137	183	167
154	138	184	168
155	139	185	169
156	140	186	170
157	141	187	171
158	142	188	172
159	143	189	173
160	144	190	174
161	145	191	175
162	146	192	176
163	147	193	177
164	148	194	178
165	149	195	179
166	150	196	180
167	151	197	181
168	152	198	182
169	153	199	183

Your 10k time is 45 minutes. You did the CHR test. You will find your personal MHR right next to your CHR:

CHR	MHR		CHR	MHR
140	123		170	153
141	124		171	154
142	125		172	155
143	126		173	156
144	127		174	157
145	128		175	158
146	129		176	159
147	130		177	160
148	131		178	161
149	132		179	162
150	133		180	163
151	134		181	164
152	135		182	165
153	136		183	166
154	137		184	167
155	138		185	168
156	139		186	169
157	140		187	170
158	141		188	171
159	142		189	172
160	143		190	173
161	144		191	174
162	145		192	175
163	146		193	176
164	147		194	177
165	148		195	178
166	149		196	179
167	150		197	180
168	151		198	181
169	152		199	182

Table header: Your 10k time is 45

Your 10k time is 46 minutes. You did the CHR test. You will find your personal MHR right next to your CHR:

	Your 10k time is 46			
CHR	MHR		CHR	MHR
140	122		170	152
141	123		171	153
142	124		172	154
143	125		173	155
144	126		174	156
145	127		175	157
146	128		176	158
147	129		177	159
148	130		178	160
149	131		179	161
150	132		180	162
151	133		181	163
152	134		182	164
153	135		183	165
154	136		184	166
155	137		185	167
156	138		186	168
157	139		187	169
158	140		188	170
159	141		189	171
160	142		190	172
161	143		191	173
162	144		192	174
163	145		193	175
164	146		194	176
165	147		195	177
166	148		196	178
167	149		197	179
168	150		198	180
169	151		199	181

Your 10k time is 47 minutes. You did the CHR test. You will find your personal MHR right next to your CHR:

	Your 10k time is			
	47			
CHR	**MHR**		**CHR**	**MHR**
140	121		170	151
141	122		171	152
142	123		172	153
143	124		173	154
144	125		174	155
145	126		175	156
146	127		176	157
147	128		177	158
148	129		178	159
149	130		179	160
150	131		180	161
151	132		181	162
152	133		182	163
153	134		183	164
154	135		184	165
155	136		185	166
156	137		186	167
157	138		187	168
158	139		188	169
159	140		189	170
160	141		190	171
161	142		191	172
162	143		192	173
163	144		193	174
164	145		194	175
165	146		195	176
166	147		196	177
167	148		197	178
168	149		198	179
169	150		199	180

Your 10k time is 48 minutes. You did the CHR test. You will find your personal MHR right next to your CHR:

Your 10k time is				
48				
CHR	MHR		CHR	MHR
140	120		170	150
141	121		171	151
142	122		172	152
143	123		173	153
144	124		174	154
145	125		175	155
146	126		176	156
147	127		177	157
148	128		178	158
149	129		179	159
150	130		180	160
151	131		181	161
152	132		182	162
153	133		183	163
154	134		184	164
155	135		185	165
156	136		186	166
157	137		187	167
158	138		188	168
159	139		189	169
160	140		190	170
161	141		191	171
162	142		192	172
163	143		193	173
164	144		194	174
165	145		195	175
166	146		196	176
167	147		197	177
168	148		198	178
169	149		199	179

Your 10k time is 49 minutes. You did the CHR test. You will find your personal MHR right next to your CHR:

Your 10k time is				
49				
CHR	**MHR**		**CHR**	**MHR**
140	119		170	149
141	120		171	150
142	121		172	151
143	122		173	152
144	123		174	153
145	124		175	154
146	125		176	155
147	126		177	156
148	127		178	157
149	128		179	158
150	129		180	159
151	130		181	160
152	131		182	161
153	132		183	162
154	133		184	163
155	134		185	164
156	135		186	165
157	136		187	166
158	137		188	167
159	138		189	168
160	139		190	169
161	140		191	170
162	141		192	171
163	142		193	172
164	143		194	173
165	144		195	174
166	145		196	175
167	146		197	176
168	147		198	177
169	148		199	178

Your 10k time is 50 minutes. You did the CHR test. You will find your personal MHR right next to your CHR:

Your 10k time is				
50				
CHR	MHR		CHR	MHR
140	118		170	148
141	119		171	149
142	120		172	150
143	121		173	151
144	122		174	152
145	123		175	153
146	124		176	154
147	125		177	155
148	126		178	156
149	127		179	157
150	128		180	158
151	129		181	159
152	130		182	160
153	131		183	161
154	132		184	162
155	133		185	163
156	134		186	164
157	135		187	165
158	136		188	166
159	137		189	167
160	138		190	168
161	139		191	169
162	140		192	170
163	141		193	171
164	142		194	172
165	143		195	173
166	144		196	174
167	145		197	175
168	146		198	176
169	147		199	177

Your 10k time is 51 minutes. You did the CHR test. You will find your personal MHR right next to your CHR:

Your 10k time is				
51				
CHR	MHR		CHR	MHR
140	117		170	147
141	118		171	148
142	119		172	149
143	120		173	150
144	121		174	151
145	122		175	152
146	123		176	153
147	124		177	154
148	125		178	155
149	126		179	156
150	127		180	157
151	128		181	158
152	129		182	159
153	130		183	160
154	131		184	161
155	132		185	162
156	133		186	163
157	134		187	164
158	135		188	165
159	136		189	166
160	137		190	167
161	138		191	168
162	139		192	169
163	140		193	170
164	141		194	171
165	142		195	172
166	143		196	173
167	144		197	174
168	145		198	175
169	146		199	176

Your 10k time is 52 minutes. You did the CHR test. You will find your personal MHR right next to your CHR:

	Your 10k time is			
	52			
CHR	**MHR**		**CHR**	**MHR**
140	116		170	146
141	117		171	147
142	118		172	148
143	119		173	149
144	120		174	150
145	121		175	151
146	122		176	152
147	123		177	153
148	124		178	154
149	125		179	155
150	126		180	156
151	127		181	157
152	128		182	158
153	129		183	159
154	130		184	160
155	131		185	161
156	132		186	162
157	133		187	163
158	134		188	164
159	135		189	165
160	136		190	166
161	137		191	167
162	138		192	168
163	139		193	169
164	140		194	170
165	141		195	171
166	142		196	172
167	143		197	173
168	144		198	174
169	145		199	175

Your 10k time is 53 minutes. You did the CHR test. You will find your personal MHR right next to your CHR:

Your 10k time is			
53			
CHR	MHR	CHR	MHR
140	115	170	145
141	116	171	146
142	117	172	147
143	118	173	148
144	119	174	149
145	120	175	150
146	121	176	151
147	122	177	152
148	123	178	153
149	124	179	154
150	125	180	155
151	126	181	156
152	127	182	157
153	128	183	158
154	129	184	159
155	130	185	160
156	131	186	161
157	132	187	162
158	133	188	163
159	134	189	164
160	135	190	165
161	136	191	166
162	137	192	167
163	138	193	168
164	139	194	169
165	140	195	170
166	141	196	171
167	142	197	172
168	143	198	173
169	144	199	174

Your 10k time is 54 minutes. You did the CHR test. You will find your personal MHR right next to your CHR:

	Your 10k time is			
	54			
CHR	MHR		CHR	MHR
140	114		170	144
141	115		171	145
142	116		172	146
143	117		173	147
144	118		174	148
145	119		175	149
146	120		176	150
147	121		177	151
148	122		178	152
149	123		179	153
150	124		180	154
151	125		181	155
152	126		182	156
153	127		183	157
154	128		184	158
155	129		185	159
156	130		186	160
157	131		187	161
158	132		188	162
159	133		189	163
160	134		190	164
161	135		191	165
162	136		192	166
163	137		193	167
164	138		194	168
165	139		195	169
166	140		196	170
167	141		197	171
168	142		198	172
169	143		199	173

Your 10k time is 55 minutes. You did the CHR test. You will find your personal MHR right next to your CHR:

Your 10k time is 55			
CHR	MHR	CHR	MHR
140	113	170	143
141	114	171	144
142	115	172	145
143	116	173	146
144	117	174	147
145	118	175	148
146	119	176	149
147	120	177	150
148	121	178	151
149	122	179	152
150	123	180	153
151	124	181	154
152	125	182	155
153	126	183	156
154	127	184	157
155	128	185	158
156	129	186	159
157	130	187	160
158	131	188	161
159	132	189	162
160	133	190	163
161	134	191	164
162	135	192	165
163	136	193	166
164	137	194	167
165	138	195	168
166	139	196	169
167	140	197	170
168	141	198	171
169	142	199	172

Your 10k time is 56 minutes. You did the CHR test. You will find your personal MHR right next to your CHR:

Your 10k time is				
56				
CHR	MHR		CHR	MHR
140	112		170	142
141	113		171	143
142	114		172	144
143	115		173	145
144	116		174	146
145	117		175	147
146	118		176	148
147	119		177	149
148	120		178	150
149	121		179	151
150	122		180	152
151	123		181	153
152	124		182	154
153	125		183	155
154	126		184	156
155	127		185	157
156	128		186	158
157	129		187	159
158	130		188	160
159	131		189	161
160	132		190	162
161	133		191	163
162	134		192	164
163	135		193	165
164	136		194	166
165	137		195	167
166	138		196	168
167	139		197	169
168	140		198	170
169	141		199	171

Your 10k time is 57 minutes. You did the CHR test. You will find your personal MHR right next to your CHR:

Your 10k time is			
57			
CHR	**MHR**	**CHR**	**MHR**
140	111	170	141
141	112	171	142
142	113	172	143
143	114	173	144
144	115	174	145
145	116	175	146
146	117	176	147
147	118	177	148
148	119	178	149
149	120	179	150
150	121	180	151
151	122	181	152
152	123	182	153
153	124	183	154
154	125	184	155
155	126	185	156
156	127	186	157
157	128	187	158
158	129	188	159
159	130	189	160
160	131	190	161
161	132	191	162
162	133	192	163
163	134	193	164
164	135	194	165
165	136	195	166
166	137	196	167
167	138	197	168
168	139	198	169
169	140	199	170

Your 10k time is 58 minutes. You did the CHR test. You will find your personal MHR right next to your CHR:

Your 10k time is 58			
CHR	MHR	CHR	MHR
140	110	170	140
141	111	171	141
142	112	172	142
143	113	173	143
144	114	174	144
145	115	175	145
146	116	176	146
147	117	177	147
148	118	178	148
149	119	179	149
150	120	180	150
151	121	181	151
152	122	182	152
153	123	183	153
154	124	184	154
155	125	185	155
156	126	186	156
157	127	187	157
158	128	188	158
159	129	189	159
160	130	190	160
161	131	191	161
162	132	192	162
163	133	193	163
164	134	194	164
165	135	195	165
166	136	196	166
167	137	197	167
168	138	198	168
169	139	199	169

Your 10k time is 59 minutes. You did the CHR test. You will find your personal MHR right next to your CHR:

CHR	MHR		CHR	MHR
	Your 10k time is			
	59			
CHR	**MHR**		**CHR**	**MHR**
140	109		170	139
141	110		171	140
142	111		172	141
143	112		173	142
144	113		174	143
145	114		175	144
146	115		176	145
147	116		177	146
148	117		178	147
149	118		179	148
150	119		180	149
151	120		181	150
152	121		182	151
153	122		183	152
154	123		184	153
155	124		185	154
156	125		186	155
157	126		187	156
158	127		188	157
159	128		189	158
160	129		190	159
161	130		191	160
162	131		192	161
163	132		193	162
164	133		194	163
165	134		195	164
166	135		196	165
167	136		197	166
168	137		198	167
169	138		199	168

Your 10k time is 60 minutes. You did the CHR test. You will find your personal MHR right next to your CHR:

	Your 10k time is				
	60				
CHR	MHR			CHR	MHR
140	108			170	138
141	109			171	139
142	110			172	140
143	111			173	141
144	112			174	142
145	113			175	143
146	114			176	144
147	115			177	145
148	116			178	146
149	117			179	147
150	118			180	148
151	119			181	149
152	120			182	150
153	121			183	151
154	122			184	152
155	123			185	153
156	124			186	154
157	125			187	155
158	126			188	156
159	127			189	157
160	128			190	158
161	129			191	159
162	130			192	160
163	131			193	161
164	132			194	162
165	133			195	163
166	134			196	164
167	135			197	165
168	136			198	166
169	137			199	167

Your 10k time is 61 minutes. You did the CHR test. You will find your personal MHR right next to your CHR:

	Your 10k time is			
	61			
CHR	MHR		CHR	MHR
140	107		170	137
141	108		171	138
142	109		172	139
143	110		173	140
144	111		174	141
145	112		175	142
146	113		176	143
147	114		177	144
148	115		178	145
149	116		179	146
150	117		180	147
151	118		181	148
152	119		182	149
153	120		183	150
154	121		184	151
155	122		185	152
156	123		186	153
157	124		187	154
158	125		188	155
159	126		189	156
160	127		190	157
161	128		191	158
162	129		192	159
163	130		193	160
164	131		194	161
165	132		195	162
166	133		196	163
167	134		197	164
168	135		198	165
169	136		199	166

Your 10k time is 62 minutes. You did the CHR test. You will find your personal MHR right next to your CHR:

Your 10k time is			
62			
CHR	MHR	CHR	MHR
140	106	170	136
141	107	171	137
142	108	172	138
143	109	173	139
144	110	174	140
145	111	175	141
146	112	176	142
147	113	177	143
148	114	178	144
149	115	179	145
150	116	180	146
151	117	181	147
152	118	182	148
153	119	183	149
154	120	184	150
155	121	185	151
156	122	186	152
157	123	187	153
158	124	188	154
159	125	189	155
160	126	190	156
161	127	191	157
162	128	192	158
163	129	193	159
164	130	194	160
165	131	195	161
166	132	196	162
167	133	197	163
168	134	198	164
169	135	199	165

Your 10k time is 63 minutes. You did the CHR test. You will find your personal MHR right next to your CHR:

Your 10k time is				
63				
CHR	**MHR**		**CHR**	**MHR**
140	105		170	135
141	106		171	136
142	107		172	137
143	108		173	138
144	109		174	139
145	110		175	140
146	111		176	141
147	112		177	142
148	113		178	143
149	114		179	144
150	115		180	145
151	116		181	146
152	117		182	147
153	118		183	148
154	119		184	149
155	120		185	150
156	121		186	151
157	122		187	152
158	123		188	153
159	124		189	154
160	125		190	155
161	126		191	156
162	127		192	157
163	128		193	158
164	129		194	159
165	130		195	160
166	131		196	161
167	132		197	162
168	133		198	163
169	134		199	164

Your 10k time is 64 minutes. You did the CHR test. You will find your personal MHR right next to your CHR:

Your 10k time is			
64			
CHR	MHR	CHR	MHR
140	104	170	134
141	105	171	135
142	106	172	136
143	107	173	137
144	108	174	138
145	109	175	139
146	110	176	140
147	111	177	141
148	112	178	142
149	113	179	143
150	114	180	144
151	115	181	145
152	116	182	146
153	117	183	147
154	118	184	148
155	119	185	149
156	120	186	150
157	121	187	151
158	122	188	152
159	123	189	153
160	124	190	154
161	125	191	155
162	126	192	156
163	127	193	157
164	128	194	158
165	129	195	159
166	130	196	160
167	131	197	161
168	132	198	162
169	133	199	163

Your 10k time is 65 minutes. You did the CHR test. You will find your personal MHR right next to your CHR:

Your 10k time is			
65			
CHR	**MHR**	**CHR**	**MHR**
140	103	170	133
141	104	171	134
142	105	172	135
143	106	173	136
144	107	174	137
145	108	175	138
146	109	176	139
147	110	177	140
148	111	178	141
149	112	179	142
150	113	180	143
151	114	181	144
152	115	182	145
153	116	183	146
154	117	184	147
155	118	185	148
156	119	186	149
157	120	187	150
158	121	188	151
159	122	189	152
160	123	190	153
161	124	191	154
162	125	192	155
163	126	193	156
164	127	194	157
165	128	195	158
166	129	196	159
167	130	197	160
168	131	198	161
169	132	199	162

Your 10k time is 66 minutes. You did the CHR test. You will find your personal MHR right next to your CHR:

Your 10k time is			
66			
CHR	MHR	CHR	MHR
140	102	170	132
141	103	171	133
142	104	172	134
143	105	173	135
144	106	174	136
145	107	175	137
146	108	176	138
147	109	177	139
148	110	178	140
149	111	179	141
150	112	180	142
151	113	181	143
152	114	182	144
153	115	183	145
154	116	184	146
155	117	185	147
156	118	186	148
157	119	187	149
158	120	188	150
159	121	189	151
160	122	190	152
161	123	191	153
162	124	192	154
163	125	193	155
164	126	194	156
165	127	195	157
166	128	196	158
167	129	197	159
168	130	198	160
169	131	199	161

Your 10k time is 67 minutes. You did the CHR test. You will find your personal MHR right next to your CHR:

Your 10k time is			
67			
CHR	MHR	CHR	MHR
140	101	170	131
141	102	171	132
142	103	172	133
143	104	173	134
144	105	174	135
145	106	175	136
146	107	176	137
147	108	177	138
148	109	178	139
149	110	179	140
150	111	180	141
151	112	181	142
152	113	182	143
153	114	183	144
154	115	184	145
155	116	185	146
156	117	186	147
157	118	187	148
158	119	188	149
159	120	189	150
160	121	190	151
161	122	191	152
162	123	192	153
163	124	193	154
164	125	194	155
165	126	195	156
166	127	196	157
167	128	197	158
168	129	198	159
169	130	199	160

Your 10k time is 68 minutes. You did the CHR test. You will find your personal MHR right next to your CHR:

Your 10k time is				
68				
CHR	**MHR**		**CHR**	**MHR**
140	100		170	130
141	101		171	131
142	102		172	132
143	103		173	133
144	104		174	134
145	105		175	135
146	106		176	136
147	107		177	137
148	108		178	138
149	109		179	139
150	110		180	140
151	111		181	141
152	112		182	142
153	113		183	143
154	114		184	144
155	115		185	145
156	116		186	146
157	117		187	147
158	118		188	148
159	119		189	149
160	120		190	150
161	121		191	151
162	122		192	152
163	123		193	153
164	124		194	154
165	125		195	155
166	126		196	156
167	127		197	157
168	128		198	158
169	129		199	159

Your 10k time is 69 minutes. You did the CHR test. You will find your personal MHR right next to your CHR:

Your 10k time is			
69			
CHR	**MHR**	**CHR**	**MHR**
140	99	170	129
141	100	171	130
142	101	172	131
143	102	173	132
144	103	174	133
145	104	175	134
146	105	176	135
147	106	177	136
148	107	178	137
149	108	179	138
150	109	180	139
151	110	181	140
152	111	182	141
153	112	183	142
154	113	184	143
155	114	185	144
156	115	186	145
157	116	187	146
158	117	188	147
159	118	189	148
160	119	190	149
161	120	191	150
162	121	192	151
163	122	193	152
164	123	194	153
165	124	195	154
166	125	196	155
167	126	197	156
168	127	198	157
169	128	199	158

Your 10k time is 70 minutes. You did the CHR test. You will find your personal MHR right next to your CHR:

Your 10k time is			
70			
CHR	**MHR**	**CHR**	**MHR**
140	98	170	128
141	99	171	129
142	100	172	130
143	101	173	131
144	102	174	132
145	103	175	133
146	104	176	134
147	105	177	135
148	106	178	136
149	107	179	137
150	108	180	138
151	109	181	139
152	110	182	140
153	111	183	141
154	112	184	142
155	113	185	143
156	114	186	144
157	115	187	145
158	116	188	146
159	117	189	147
160	118	190	148
161	119	191	149
162	120	192	150
163	121	193	151
164	122	194	152
165	123	195	153
166	124	196	154
167	125	197	155
168	126	198	156
169	127	199	157

Your 10k time is 71 minutes. You did the CHR test. You will find your personal MHR right next to your CHR:

Your 10k time is			
71			
CHR	MHR	CHR	MHR
140	97	170	127
141	98	171	128
142	99	172	129
143	100	173	130
144	101	174	131
145	102	175	132
146	103	176	133
147	104	177	134
148	105	178	135
149	106	179	136
150	107	180	137
151	108	181	138
152	109	182	139
153	110	183	140
154	111	184	141
155	112	185	142
156	113	186	143
157	114	187	144
158	115	188	145
159	116	189	146
160	117	190	147
161	118	191	148
162	119	192	149
163	120	193	150
164	121	194	151
165	122	195	152
166	123	196	153
167	124	197	154
168	125	198	155
169	126	199	156

Your 10k time is 72 minutes. You did the CHR test. You will find your personal MHR right next to your CHR:

Your 10k time is				
72				
CHR	MHR		CHR	MHR
140	96		170	126
141	97		171	127
142	98		172	128
143	99		173	129
144	100		174	130
145	101		175	131
146	102		176	132
147	103		177	133
148	104		178	134
149	105		179	135
150	106		180	136
151	107		181	137
152	108		182	138
153	109		183	139
154	110		184	140
155	111		185	141
156	112		186	142
157	113		187	143
158	114		188	144
159	115		189	145
160	116		190	146
161	117		191	147
162	118		192	148
163	119		193	149
164	120		194	150
165	121		195	151
166	122		196	152
167	123		197	153
168	124		198	154
169	125		199	155

Your 10k time is 73 minutes. You did the CHR test. You will find your personal MHR right next to your CHR:

Your 10k time is				
73				
CHR	MHR		CHR	MHR
140	95		170	125
141	96		171	126
142	97		172	127
143	98		173	128
144	99		174	129
145	100		175	130
146	101		176	131
147	102		177	132
148	103		178	133
149	104		179	134
150	105		180	135
151	106		181	136
152	107		182	137
153	108		183	138
154	109		184	139
155	110		185	140
156	111		186	141
157	112		187	142
158	113		188	143
159	114		189	144
160	115		190	145
161	116		191	146
162	117		192	147
163	118		193	148
164	119		194	149
165	120		195	150
166	121		196	151
167	122		197	152
168	123		198	153
169	124		199	154

Your 10k time is 74 minutes. You did the CHR test. You will find your personal MHR right next to your CHR:

Your 10k time is			
74			
CHR	MHR	CHR	MHR
140	94	170	124
141	95	171	125
142	96	172	126
143	97	173	127
144	98	174	128
145	99	175	129
146	100	176	130
147	101	177	131
148	102	178	132
149	103	179	133
150	104	180	134
151	105	181	135
152	106	182	136
153	107	183	137
154	108	184	138
155	109	185	139
156	110	186	140
157	111	187	141
158	112	188	142
159	113	189	143
160	114	190	144
161	115	191	145
162	116	192	146
163	117	193	147
164	118	194	148
165	119	195	149
166	120	196	150
167	121	197	151
168	122	198	152
169	123	199	153

Your 10k time is 75 minutes. You did the CHR test. You will find your personal MHR right next to your CHR:

	Your 10k time is		
	75		
CHR	MHR	CHR	MHR
140	93	170	123
141	94	171	124
142	95	172	125
143	96	173	126
144	97	174	127
145	98	175	128
146	99	176	129
147	100	177	130
148	101	178	131
149	102	179	132
150	103	180	133
151	104	181	134
152	105	182	135
153	106	183	136
154	107	184	137
155	108	185	138
156	109	186	139
157	110	187	140
158	111	188	141
159	112	189	142
160	113	190	143
161	114	191	144
162	115	192	145
163	116	193	146
164	117	194	147
165	118	195	148
166	119	196	149
167	120	197	150
168	121	198	151
169	122	199	152

11. FINISH TIME PREDICTED

In the previous chapter we have used your best 10k time to define your MHR. Now we use the same personal best 10k time to predict your marathon end time, if you run at the calculated MHR. In fact, with your 10k time and your MHR we find your personal running pace 'sweat spot' that will lead you to the predicted marathon finish time.

The predicted marathon finish time, while running at your MHR, is quite accurate. To most runners it is like +/- 5 minutes.

Also, with this table, it is easy to determine if someone's marathon finish time goal is realistic or not.

"Last year I ran a marathon just below 5 hours. This year my goal is 4h30"!

This type of goal setting I hear very often. With the CHR test and a recent 10k time it is easy to figure out if this person's goal is realistic.

The above also implicates that -for someone who really has an over-optimistic marathon finish time goal- the first objective should be to substantially improve his or hers' 10k time. The reality is that -if this person can't make the required time improvement on the 10k- the desired marathon finish time is just a fantasy as well. Your best 10k effort and your (potential) marathon finish time are connected like my 2 beautiful twin-girls.

A substantial improvement on your 10k time means you can start dreaming of a new, realistic, substantially quicker marathon finish time goal as well. So you can use the months in between marathons to focus on a 10k or half marathon. It is not just for variation or fun; it is an easy step-up towards achieving your marathon goals.

In the table below you will find a listing of 10k finish times. The marathon finish time predictions are linked to the 10k finish times. The 10k <-> 42k extrapolations are based on my own experiences with my running students, supported by the findings of Stans van der Poel. They are not based on the empirical extrapolations applied to the elite and professional athletes, such as Runner's World and Sate's are publishing. I found that for age-group runners these tables are over-ambitious. The Vickers system comes closer to my own prediction times but I still think it's too ambitious and will lead to disappointment and frustration.

Please take a margin of the predicted marathon finish times of +/- 5 minutes into account.

For those of you who run your 10k between 65 and 75 minutes, the 9-Mile Marathon training system is applicable, but I propose that you add a walk of 60 seconds EVERY mile in all of your MHR training runs AND your race. You can combine the walks with grabbing a drink or a bite at the water posts. When you walk every mile for a minute you add 26 minutes to your predicted finish time. So, when your 10k time is between 1h05 and 1h15, your MHR running pace remains 12:35 min/mile, and your predicted finish time will be around 6 hours. You will get faster when you decrease your walk time to f.i. 50s or 40s.

10k finish time	predicted marathon finish time	required marathon pace min/k	required marathon pace min/mile
1h05	5h30	7:49	12:35
1h03	5h22	7:37	12:17
1h01	5h14	7:26	11:59
59:00	5h06	7:15	11:40
57:00	4h58	7:03	11:22
55:00	4h50	6:52	11:04
54:00	4h42	6:40	10:45
53:00	4h34	6:29	10:27
52:00	4h26	6:18	10:09
51:00	4h18	6:06	9:50
50:00	4h10	5:55	9:32
49:00	4h02	5:44	9:14
48:00	3h56	5:35	9:00
47:00	3h50	5:27	8:46
46:00	3h44	5:18	8:32
45:00	3h39	5:11	8:21
44:00	3h33	5:02	8:07
43:00	3h28	4:55	7:56
42:00	3h23	4:48	7:44
41:00	3h18	4:42	7:35
40:00	3h14	4:37	7:26
39:15	3h10	4:30	7:15
38:30	3h06	4:24	7:05
37:45	3h02	4:18	6:56
37:00	2h58	4:13	6:47

FINISH TIME PREDICTION TABLE 1
MARATHON Training on MHR pace

12. THE 9-MILE MARATHON SCHEDULE

In the regular, classic high mileage-based training schedules (as they are still very popular) there is an almost certain 100% probability of fatigue accumulation for average age-group runners.

In order to prepare yourself for a marathon, I found in 2015 while training for the Ironman 70.3 World Championship, backed by the research of Stans van der Poel, it is far more efficient to frequently train 75-90 minutes medium- long runs at marathon heart rate MHR rather than weekly high mileage high wear-and-tear low hr, slow long runs. Even more so, in the past, the Verheul method taught us to pay a lot of attention to full recovery interval speedwork, strength training and Fartlek running (an unstructured running workout, play with speed), which requires a certain loose attitude.

Both van der Poel and Verheul thus representing a quite different approach from the high-milage based classic training methodology.

In 2015 and 2016 hundreds of Dutch runners who followed the disruptive ideas of Stans van der Poel completed their marathons happy, healthy and without injuries.

The 9-Mile Marathon program is built on my personal life-long experience with high level endurance training and racing, my experiences in 2014 and 2015 as I described in the early chapters of this book, my classes and coaching experiences, Stans' scientific foundation of frequent medium long runs at marathon speed and the Verheul method as a comprehensive training program.

As a coherent package, besides the medium long runs at MHR twice per week, The 9-Mile Marathon training program emphasizes:

1- One weekly speed training (interval) to prepare and to 'harden' yourself for the tough final miles;

2- Cross training, or any easy AYF- (as-you-feel) run, at least once per week: physically, mentally and emotionally highly recommended (body pump, spinning, yoga, etc..);

3- Strength endurance training (focus on planking and squats) for core stability (Please check the "ADD-ON" on how to do the right core stability and strength training);

4- Breathing technique to optimize the supply of O2 during the day and while running.

The 9-Mile Marathon schedule runs 90 days. There are three fundamental runs per week, of which two are somewhat longer runs and one speed/interval run.

As a fixed part of your weekly schedule I want you to do one cross training, like body pump, spinning or yoga, and 2-3 times per week 10-15 minutes of strength endurance training with the focus on core strength, planking and squats (no weights, high number of reps).

9miler4life.com

When, during the week, you would like to do an additional easy as-you-feel (AYF) run like 3-5 miles at MHR with a couple of 10 second speed-ups, The 9-Mile Marathon schedule allows that too. If you opt for an AYF run this run will then be the substitute for your weekly cross training. So it's either/or Cross/ AYF.

The maximum long run in the 90-Day prep program is 9 miles (14k). In the beginning of the 90-Day program the 'long runs' even starts with just 5 or 6 miles.

In The 9-Mile Marathon program, one training per week is Speed/Interval training. In the Speed/Interval reps you run faster than your marathon running speed at MHR. Please check the "ADD-ON" on how to do the right Speed/Interval training. I have put a 6 interval sets together who are specifically tailored for The 9-Mile Marathon training program you will find in the 'SPEED' add-on guide.

On the long runs you run as close as possible to your MHR. Your running pace may vary; it will depend on many variables like the outside temperature or a hilly or windy course. Your MHR, however, will always be the same. On a hot day, you run at your MHR and your speed will be lower than normal as a result of the higher temperatures. Same with humidity. Or altitude. When you run a hilly course you slow down going up and speed up a little going down. Always try to stay as close to your MHR as possible. On a windy day, your stretches against the wind will slow you down to keep your MHR spot on.

The 9-Mile Marathon schedule starts on a Sunday because most marathons are scheduled on Sundays. When your marathon is on Saturday or another day of the week you compensate in the final "relaxation" week by skipping one or two days of rest of your very low intensity final run.

The final training week is the week before race day. So we are talking about a prep period of 12+1 week minus race day; 90 days altogether. Your last scheduled training will be on the Friday before race day. On the Saturday before race day you just try to relax or put on your running shoes and enjoy a 12-20 minute jog to get rid of your nerves ;-).

The 9-Mile Marathon schedule gives you lots of freedom to integrate your running related activities into your weekly busy schedule. The schedule is designed to be less rigid. I'm not a fan of those overly detailed, structured, rigid schedules. To put in other words:

Get Rid Of The Rigid!

What I basically give you is four Blocks of 3 training weeks with a certain 'rhythm'. Plus a 'FINAL WEEK' schedule. All Blocks start on Sunday.

The first 3 Weeks Block (Block 1):

1- Sundays: MHR long run of 5-6 miles

2- During the week: one regular Speed/Interval training

3- Thursdays or Fridays: MHR long run of 5-6 miles

Repeat this cycle for the upcoming 2 weeks.

The second 3 Weeks Block (Block 2):

1- Starts with something different on Sundays: a 10k race or a 6 miles run (as fast as you want to go)

2- During the week: one regular Speed/Interval training

3- Thursday or Fridays: MHR long run of 6-7 miles

The following 'regular' Sunday is a MHR 6-7 miles long run; then repeat the cycle for the next 2 weeks.

Third 3 Weeks Block (Block 3):

1- Starts again with something different on Sundays: 10k race or 6 miles run above MHR. Or, when you really want, feel free to run a half marathon at MHR.

2- During the week: one regular Speed/Interval training

3- Thursdays or Fridays: MHR long run of 7-8 miles

The following 'regular' Sundays MHR 7-8 miles long run and repeat cycle again for the next 2 weeks.

Fourth & final 3 Weeks Block (Block 4):

1- Starts again with some speed work on Sundays: 10k race or a fast 6 miles run

2- During the week: regular Speed/Interval training

3- Thursday or Fridays: MHR long run of 9 miles

The following 'regular' Sundays you do your MHR 9-mile long run. Then repeat this cycle again for the next 2 weeks.

In this final 3 Weeks Block (Block 4) you are free to cut or to extend one or two of the 9-mile runs with 1 or 2 miles.

In the Final Week before race day:

9miler4life.com

1- Sunday: 6-8 mile MHR long run including six moderate 20 seconds easy speed ups

2- During the week: easy 1 mile MHR followed by 6 times 300m just above MHR (walk or slowly dribble 150m between the 300 m's) and 1 mile MHR cool down

3- No more strength, no more cross training, no more speedwork

4- Friday: 2-3 miles MHR run including 6 moderate 20 second speed-ups

5- Saturday: If you want to, put on your shoes, dribble, do some less-than-0.5-mile MHR intervals, AYF, NO intensity, NO speed, NO stress

By the way, if you have to skip a training for any reason, do NOT try to catch up in the same week. Don't do this training later on. Just leave it be.

It is also very helpful to keep notes of all your trainings. Date, time, type of training, miles, minutes, total miles and minutes so far, circumstances, perceived effort, and remarks or notes.

9miler4life.com

Cross training, AYF and strength training I consider as active recovery for your marathon running program. You can move and swap trainings during the week as you feel needed. As long as there is always one day of active recovery (i.e. cross training, AYF or strength training) between either two consecutive MHR runs or MHR runs and Speedwork. Avoid daily back-to-back MHR runs and back-to-back MHR - Speedwork.

So if you want to make changes to the suggested week-by-week schedules, always schedule one day of active recovery (strength, AYF or cross training) between days with MHR runs and Speedwork runs.

Now check the tables on the following pages. The schedules as presented are an example of how you could plan your 4 blocks of 3 weeks. See how you can fit and adapt the schedules into your own day-to-day life. In the full online training program you will find a workbook with 'empty' tables to schedule your own personal plan.

9miler4life.com

THE 9-MILE MARATHON TRAINING SCHEDULE
BLOCK 1   WEEK 1, 2, 3

WEEK 1	MHR run	SPEED	CROSS/RUN	STRENGTH
SUNDAY	5-6 mile			
MONDAY				PLANK-PUSH
TUESDAY		INTERVAL 1		
WEDNESDAY				PUSH-SQUAT
THURSDAY	5-6 mile			
FRIDAY				SQUAT-PLANK
SATURDAY			AYF	

WEEK 2	MHR run	SPEED	CROSS/RUN	STRENGTH
SUNDAY	5-6 mile			
MONDAY				PLANK-PUSH
TUESDAY		INTERVAL 2		
WEDNESDAY				PUSH-SQUAT
THURSDAY	5-6 mile			
FRIDAY				SQUAT-PLANK
SATURDAY			AYF	

WEEK 3	MHR run	SPEED	CROSS/RUN	STRENGTH
SUNDAY	5-6 mile			
MONDAY				PLANK-PUSH
TUESDAY		INTERVAL 3		
WEDNESDAY				PUSH-SQUAT
THURSDAY	5-6 mile			
FRIDAY				SQUAT-PLANK
SATURDAY			AYF	

Notes:

THE 9-MILE MARATHON TRAINING SCHEDULE
BLOCK 2   **WEEK 4, 5, 6**

WEEK 4	MHR run	SPEED	CROSS/RUN	STRENGTH
SUNDAY		10k RACE		
MONDAY				PLANK
TUESDAY		INTERVAL 4		
WEDNESDAY				PUSH UP
THURSDAY	6-7 mile			
FRIDAY				SQUAT
SATURDAY			AYF	

WEEK 5	MHR run	SPEED	CROSS/RUN	STRENGTH
SUNDAY	6-7 mile			
MONDAY				PLANK
TUESDAY		INTERVAL 5		
WEDNESDAY				PUSH UP
THURSDAY	6-7 mile			
FRIDAY				SQUAT
SATURDAY			AYF	

WEEK 6	MHR run	SPEED	CROSS/RUN	STRENGTH
SUNDAY	6-7 mile			
MONDAY				PLANK
TUESDAY		INTERVAL 6		
WEDNESDAY				PUSH UP
THURSDAY	6-7 mile			
FRIDAY				SQUAT
SATURDAY			AYF	

Notes

THE 9-MILE MARATHON TRAINING SCHEDULE
BLOCK 3   WEEK 7, 8, 9

WEEK 7	MHR run	SPEED	CROSS/RUN	STRENGTH
SUNDAY	half MHR marathon or 10k race			
MONDAY				PLANK
TUESDAY		INTERVAL 1		
WEDNESDAY				PUSH UP
THURSDAY	7-8 mile			
FRIDAY				SQUAT
SATURDAY			AYF	

WEEK 8	MHR run	SPEED	CROSS/RUN	STRENGTH
SUNDAY	7-8 mile			
MONDAY				PLANK
TUESDAY		INTERVAL 2		
WEDNESDAY				PUSH UP
THURSDAY	7-8 mile			
FRIDAY				SQUAT
SATURDAY			AYF	

WEEK 9	MHR run	SPEED	CROSS/RUN	STRENGTH
SUNDAY	7-8 mile			
MONDAY				PLANK
TUESDAY		INTERVAL 3		
WEDNESDAY				PUSH UP
THURSDAY	7-8 mile			
FRIDAY				SQUAT
SATURDAY			AYF	

Notes

THE 9-MILE MARATHON TRAINING SCHEDULE
BLOCK 4   WEEK 10, 11, 12

WEEK 10	MHR run	SPEED	CROSS/RUN	STRENGTH
SUNDAY	10k race or 9 mile MHR run			
MONDAY				PLANK
TUESDAY		INTERVAL 4		
WEDNESDAY				PUSH UP
THURSDAY	9 miler			
FRIDAY				SQUAT
SATURDAY			AYF	

WEEK 11	MHR run	SPEED	CROSS/RUN	STRENGTH
SUNDAY	9 miler			
MONDAY				PLANK
TUESDAY		INTERVAL 5		
WEDNESDAY				PUSH UP
THURSDAY	9 miler			
FRIDAY				SQUAT
SATURDAY			AYF	

WEEK 12	MHR run	SPEED	CROSS/RUN	STRENGTH
SUNDAY	9 miler			
MONDAY				PLANK
TUESDAY		INTERVAL 6		
WEDNESDAY				PUSH UP
THURSDAY	9 miler			
FRIDAY				SQUAT
SATURDAY			AYF	

FINAL WEEK	MHR run	SPEED	CROSS/RUN	STRENGTH
SUNDAY	6-8 miler	With 6 moderate 20s speed ups		
MONDAY				
TUESDAY				
WEDNESDAY	3-4 mile	With 6x300 easy speed ups		
THURSDAY				
FRIDAY	2 miles	With 6 moderate 20s speed ups		
SATURDAY			AYF	
RACEDAY	RACE			

13. HOW TO RUN AT YOUR MHR

In The 9-Mile Marathon you run medium-long 5-9 mile runs at your personal MHR twice a week. These runs are the cornerstone of The 9-Mile Marathon program. It is essential to execute them well.

This is how I think you can do this best.

When your MHR is, for example, 140bpm, put an alarm on your watch at 142bpm. Personally I like to use the alarm because this way I don't need to look down and visually check my heart rate all the time.

When I am going too fast and my heart rate reaches 142, the alarm will go off to tell me to slow down a bit.

What I do next is I start to dribble (slow running at a 13 min/mile (8 min/k) pace for about half a minute. Get something to drink, as if there was a water station at this point.

Once the 30 seconds are gone I slowly accelerate back to a heart rate that is slightly lower than at the pace I ran just before the moment my watch told me to slow down. In this example, something like 136-138bpm. From here I settle at this pace; at this 'feel' I free my mind and forget about the watch, figures and facts. And just run!

When you get more experienced you will be able to run longer distances closer to your MHR. Even when you go uphill or when you run against the wind you will be able to naturally adjust your running speed and stay close to your MHR. You will develop a real 'feel' for your MHR and there will be fewer moments you will need to slow down. Experienced 9-Mile Marathon runners are able to run at least half the run without any alarm going off whatsoever. I even know of runners who are able to complete their 8-9 mile run within four +/- heartbeats of their MHR without constantly looking at their watch!

Next step is you put your watch on, but you put the sound of. During your run you just focus on the feel and your pace. Only after the run, at home, you check your run and your heart rates. In most cases you'll find that you were pretty close to your MHR. Or, you can remember exactly when you were going too fast or too slow. I'd propose in training Blocks 2 and 3 to run at least every other MHR run this way. In Block 4, the final 3-week block, you put the sound back on while running. I am pretty sure you will be able to pace yourself so well you won't hear the alarm go off more than just once or twice per run!

When you do your interval training I recommend not setting any alarm and running freely. Of course you can check your heart rate every now and then during the intervals to see what's going on. This way you will develop a sense for which heart rate is linked to which feeling at higher intensity levels.

At race day it will pay off. Because race day is different, expect to see higher heart rates at the first 1 or 2 miles due to the excitement of the event. You will probably go too fast. Don't panic! Because you have taught yourself a 'feel' for speed at the interval trainings, you will be able to quickly notice you're running too fast. Your body now recognizes this feeling. Plenty of time to tune back and to find the pace, the rhythm and the 'feel' with which you're familiar.

The same applies to the final miles of the marathon. When you feel alright don't be afraid to run above your MHR. This is what I have experienced to be normal and natural. You know you've done most of the job, and, if you still feel ok, you can loosen up and let things go a little. Two of my students had this feeling and even accelerated during the final miles. Simply because they felt they could. A wonderful experience!

14. NUTRITION

Nutrition is essential. There are many folks and specialists out there who tell you what's right for you. So what I will do right now is to share my personal thoughts about good nutrition for endurance athletes.

For The 9-Mile Marathon specific MHR and H-MHR trainings: within 2 hours before the training try not to eat at all. Early morning runs: just a little juice, water, a cup of tea.

If you really need something to eat before your training, a light toast with a little marmalade, half a banana.

A coffee before training with a little sugar? Why not.

During all types of 9-Mile Marathon training: water with electrolytes when it's hot. No energy drinks, no sugars. No gels. Do not stuff yourself with sugars right after training, either. When you desperately need some carbs after you're done, try the slow ones like oats.

Food in general. Not too many carbs. Today my daily intake (in calories) is at around 1/3 carbs, 1/3 proteins and 1/3 fats. That's a lot of fats, relatively. Why? ESS does the job. No more sugar cravings. Snack: a variety of nuts. Mind 100 grams of nuts is approx. 500 calories. Most from proteins and fats. Which is a lot. Good examples of fat and protein-rich food: whole wheat bread with real butter, peanut butter and slices of avocado. Grilled chicken breast with mayonnaise, whole cheese, green walnut, pecan, macadamia, honey, olive- salad, oily fish and pasta with white fish, fresh vegetable sauce (cabbage, beets, tomatoes, peppers, zucchini, beans, salt, pepper, basil, olive oil). A handful of mixed nuts and raisins, full-fat yoghurt with coconut, apple, mango, banana, honey, dried fruits.

Limit or delete refined sugars. Limit or delete refined and processed food. "If you can't read it, better not eat it". Too many fruit, fruit juices and smoothies contain lots of sugars as well. If you want a smoothie blend it yourself. Same with (pasta) sauces, just blend tomato, red pepper, olives, garlic, pepper, Italian herbs, basil, olive oil, some water. Take time to cook. Slow is healthy.

Don't be afraid to add healthy, unsaturated fats to your meals like olive oil, rice oil, oil from seeds.

Focus on sufficient proteins from fish, meat, vegetables, nuts, etc..

If you eat carbs, take the slow ones. Whole oats, not-completely-white pasta's, brown rice, multi-(whole-)grains bread.

Before race day: drink lots of water and eat the way you are used to. No pasta parties. Don't eat too late in the evening. Your body needs time to fully digest and process.

On race day, before the start: drink. Eat light carbs, but not within 2 hours before the race. Be very careful with proteins and fats. When you take carbs, take slow carbs like overnight oatmeal.

And now here is the little secret: During the race at mile 3, 8, 13, 18 and 23, you take one gel with 30-40 grams of carbs. Yes. Really. But only on race day! Test your gels out during one or two of your 9-mile long runs. Drink water at the aid stations. Take 10-15 seconds to make sure you drink. When you get tired just walk for a moment to be able to drink well. It will pay off.

Right after the race and the following one or two days: keep eating and drinking. Anything you like. Whatever you need. Proteins. Fats. Carbs. And drink!

15. 3-STAGE AND A-SYMMETRICAL BREATHING

Breathing efficiency is important. Really important. And you know what? Good breathing is most important when you're NOT running. Why? Because you spend most of your life NOT running! When you learn to breathe in a good way you will benefit from it not only while running, but even more so in every other area of your life.

There are many ideas about how you should breathe, but for me there is just one 'model' I always use. While I'm at rest and exercising. I call it 3-Stage Breathing.

It all starts with deep breathing, belly breathing or abdominal breathing. They are all the same, done by contracting the diaphragm. During this type of breathing as air enters the lungs the belly expands.

This I call the first stage. At rest, while you're in a meeting, easy walking, at work, having dinner, driving in your car, watching a movie. Breathing can be done easily through the nose; breathing in AND out.

The second breathing stage is required at medium-level intensity exercise. Initiated from the deep abdominal breathing stage you add higher-up breathing through lung expansion. While breathing is still initiated from deep down, you add the active expansion of the lungs through the muscles. Breathing in can still be done through your nose, while breathing out is most convenient through your mouth.

The third and final breathing stage is required at high-level intensity exercise. Still initiated from the deep abdominal breath, the third stage is a much higher-up breathing through active lung expansion in a higher frequency with your mouth open.

The challenge is for you to be aware of what stage you are in. For me running at MHR is second breathing stage. Interval training is third breathing stage. In many situations, once you are aware, you can go back from the third to the second breathing stage sooner than you expect. I think it's always better to bring your breath down to a slower pace, to a lower stage.

In most cases nose breathing is preferable. Emotionally breathing through your mouth is linked to panic and fear, associations with life-threatening situations. Deep breathing leads to the relief or prevention of symptoms associated with stress, high blood pressure, headache, depression, anxiety and others. Deep breathing techniques slow your heart rate down while high breathing through your mouth keeps the heart rate unnecessarily up.

Deep breathing stage 2 is what I have trained myself to maintain when I am running at MHR. When I do interval and speed training I let go and do stage 3 breathing. But I have learned to be aware, to control and to bring my breathing quickly back to stage 2 or even -after a couple of minutes- back to stage 1.

A-Symmetrical Breathing

There is another aspect to breathing while running.: symmetrical and a-symmetrical breathing. Let me explain.

So what if you would always carry a weight in one hand. Or run with a backpack slung over your right shoulder? With that weight you would start to compensate with your body, putting more stress on one side of your hips, pelvis and lower back.

With all the weight on one side, that side would become worn down, bit by bit, and lead to injury.

Always landing on the same foot at the beginning of your breathing cycle will cause the same effect. One side of your body will absorb a greater impact-force of running.

This is the case when your breathing pattern is even. Breathing IN for example 2 steps- and breath OUT also -2 steps.

When you walk around the room you can test yourself. Try to count the number of steps you take while breathing in, and the number of steps breathing out. When you are completely relaxed this may be like 3 steps inhaling and 3 exhaling.

Next time when you go out running try to be aware of your 'natural' breathing pattern. For most of us this may be 3 steps (left-right-left) breathing in and 3 steps (right-left-right) breathing out. Or 2 steps (left-right) breathe in and 2 steps (left-right) breathe out. Or, when you run faster, 2 steps (left-right) breathe in and 1 step out.

Now try to find a pattern to alter the leg (left or right) to start your breathing cycle with. You can do this with any UN-even breathing pattern, like 3 steps IN and 2 steps OUT, or 2 steps IN and 1 step OUT. For instance, when you are running slow, you could breath IN 2 steps (left-right) and breath out 3 steps (left-right-left). Once you have finished this cycle you will start the next breathing cycle with the other foot-stride.

When you are running faster you could breath IN 2 steps and breath OUT 1 step, or 1 step IN and 2 steps OUT, thus altering your breathing cycle every 3 steps.

Personally I think it is easier to inhale quicker than exhale. This means it is easier to inhale for instance 2 steps and exhale 3. But, for some, this is opposite. They prefer to inhale 3 steps and exhale 2 steps. The main thing is that you develop an UNeven pattern.

When I am running The 9-Miler way, my breathing pattern is most balanced when I am breathing 2 steps in and 2 steps out, which is an even pattern. I really wouldn't want to change this pattern because I feel very balanced, right at my MHR and marathon running speed.

I have solved this by adding after every two or three cycles of 2 steps in and 2 steps out, one extra step OUT. So basically my breathing pattern is 2 steps in, 2 steps out, 2 steps in, 2 steps out, 2 steps in, 3 steps out. This way my breathing is rhythmic while still changing foot strides every 6 to 7 steps.

So rhythmic breathing allows an evenly distributed stress on both sides of your body.

Now the greatest immediate impact stress of running, is evenly spread on both sides. But besides the fact that an odd pattern of foot-strides, exhales, and inhales keeping you injury-free, rhythmic breathing also focuses your attention on your breathing patterns, which puts your body in a position to better manage that stress, and stay healthy.

Attention and awareness of breathing has a long history in Eastern cultures: "To breathe fully is to live fully"!

With The 9-Mile Marathon training system I have exactly the same goal. Running a marathon is like living a life. It's the journey that counts.

The 9-Mile Marathon: Run Your Life.

16. 5 SQUARE PEGS

Here's the story of 5 Dutch runners who ran the 2016 Rotterdam Marathon using the training concept of Stans van der Poel. Their story was published in the Dutch RUNNER'S WORLD 2016 June edition. They call themselves' The Stone City Runners.' Klaas (51), Miranda, Diana (both 42), Niek (53) and Ysbrand (54). For Klaas, Miranda, Diana and Niek this was their first marathon, ever. Niek had run two marathons before.

First they determined their personal MHR with the test. The heart rates Stans van der Poel used were even lower than ours and based on a somewhat different formula and test sequence. But in the end they all committed to stick to the calculated heart rate.

When they started the training, to most, their speeds were quite low. They had trouble not speeding up too much. It felt slow and sometimes a bit overly relaxed. This caused doubt for some. They had to run slower than they were used to. But still, their intention was to stick to the plan.

For Diana, the training didn't go that well because of an injury, which she had from the beginning of the training. During the first weeks she had to skip trainings frequently. She didn't want to push and risk any further damage. She only managed to complete ¾ of all trainings.

Compared with 'regular' training schedules, she would have done less than 50%. That's substantially fewer miles than what's usual, especially for a first-timer. Thankfully, along the way, in the second half of the training period, she got better and she managed to run most of the scheduled trainings at the heart rate Stan's system prescribed.

Miranda, on the other hand, was able to follow the schedule very precisely. Total number of training miles, types of trainings and heart rate were close to perfection.

Klaas, Niek and Ysbrand all followed the scheduled trainings but not as precise as Miranda. Sometimes they had to skip one of the trainings because of a little pain, a cold or a busy social or work schedule. But all in all they managed to do most of the trainings according to the schedules.

Niek and Klaas couldn't always control themselves and they ran a couple of trainings faster than they should. Or they ran more than 14k, mainly in the second half of the training period. Klaas ran a couple of trainings longer than 19k (12 miles), even though he was not an experienced marathon runner. It was just that he felt he could do it, so he did. Ysbrand followed the schedule quite close and did not do any runs substantially longer than 9 miles.

For each of them the training schedule felt very good and they all stated it wasn't difficult to integrate the training program into their busy schedules.

At race day Diana finished very well, even a bit faster than expected. Although she didn't do all trainings due to her injury, the precise running at her MHR seemed to pay off. Same with Ysbrand who precisely followed MHR and the scheduled trainings during the entire training period. Ysbrand, too, managed to finish happy and healthy, ran a negative split and even a bit quicker than scheduled.

Miranda, who followed the schedule most precisely, finished almost exactly at her scheduled finish time. She didn't experience any difficulties along the way.

Niek and Klaas made the classic mistake of starting a little too fast-- inspired by the masses and the energy they felt as part of a 17,000-strong crowd. Halfway through the race they were back on track and they managed to run at the pace they maintained for most of their trainings. Toward the end of the race both Niek and Klaas had to slow down a couple of times. Maybe because of their quick start? Or maybe because of the trainings they did at a faster pace and for longer than actually scheduled?

What struck them most was the happiness they all experienced at the finish. What Niek commented was typical and immensely rewarding: "I ran six half-marathons and they all went quite heavy. I never thought I could run a full marathon this way."

Happy and healthy finishers. No major problems along the road.

You Don't Have To Play This Game Alone.

There are marathon runners, including me, who want to welcome you in The 9-Mile Tribe and support you on your Marathon Running journey.

Will You Join Us?

The Choice Is Yours.

17. WHY YOU SHOULD NOT TRAIN LIKE THE PRO'S

You are an age-group athlete right? Living a busy life with work, family, friends.

Most online training programs tell you that 'training like the pro's' is the best way to get your pr. Which is a huge mistake.

Too many age-group athletes suffer from those long training runs, both mentally and physically. Traditional high mileage training schedules are wearing you out, like boiling the frog slowly. You train harder and harder, push yourself, but your not making anyway near the progress you anticipated.

And then, after the fourth or fifth long training run.. you're stuck.

After more than 25 years of competing and coaching at the highest level, I realized this happens to 80% of all age-group runners over 40, running marathons between 3 1/2 and 5 1/2 hours.

Which is a shame..

For age-group athletes a balanced life is key to success. To me success has a different meaning. For us, non-professional running enthusiasts, our max potential lies within the context of the life we're living.

This is the question I always hear. Hey coach, I want to run my fastest marathon ever. Is The 9-Mile Marathon system the way to go?

I have developed The 9-Mile Marathon training system to allow YOU to run your best marathon at THIS particular moment in THIS particular situation. So the answer may be "YES" when your current situation allows you to perform at your best. But the answer may be "NO" when your life has been very busy with work, or with your family life that needed your attention. So I am looking at 'performance' from a different angle. When you have a busy job, running a family and living a social life, you will NEVER be able to run the fastest possible marathon of your life at the same time. With The 9-Mile Marathon training program you will run your best marathon GIVEN your personal circumstances.

I'm quoting Mat Dixon here, triathlon coach: "Ultimately, long-term sustainable success is going to require a clean slate, a new approach that permeates all areas of your busy life. The good news is that if you can take this on, you should not only achieve your [triathlon-] aspirations but also establish a platform for excelling in health, work, and life as a whole."

This is SO true! When athletes try to squeeze all their running ambitions into overloaded daily and weekly high mileage training programs then, combined with the other important commitments of life, they're heading for disaster. This is the typical self pressure of going after that PR race-after-race, pushed by the running 'peer-pressure' of training those 'casual' 50-miles per week, leading to fatigue accumulation, chronicle fatigue, injury and mental exhaustion or even burnout.

I believe in success within the context of a balanced life. Your goal can' be to break a pr, be on the podium in your age-group, qualify for Boston or even just run a little bit faster than your previous run at the cost of life! As an age-group non-pro runner, your ambitions and performance have to be based on a well balanced life that takes into account all your personal circumstances.

18. WHAT TO DO BETWEEN RACES

What can you do when the time between two races is more than 90 days? How can you 'use' this 'idle' time best -the 9-miler way?

Normally you're not running your marathons back to back. There is more time between the marathons you're running than the required 90-day prep time 'the 9-miler way'. Most of us are running two marathons per year, which means four 90-day 'blocks' of 3 months/12 weeks per year. One (3-month) 90-day block 9-mile marathon prep, followed by one (3-month) 90-day block 'idle' state. Then one more (3-month) 90-day block 9-mile marathon prep, again followed by the last 3 month 'idle' state.

So what do you do in between, during this 'idle' state time? What CAN you do between races?

My First Answer Would Be Something Like "Anything"!

Because when you train 'The 9-Miler Way', you're NOT really building towards a huge exhausting 'peak' and you don't need the next 4-6 weeks to heal and recover. When you train the 'traditional way' you need at least one month to recover both mentally and physically from the race and the traditional high wear-and-tear training period. When you train the 9-miler way, the AFA concept, the AVOIDANCE of building and accumulating fatigue, allows you to recover from your marathon QUICKER than you would if you were training the traditional way. Physically, and in particular mentally/emotionally.

To me, personally, the 'idle' time between your race and the next period of 90 days to start picking up the 9-mile program again, I use to do REALLY other things like vacation, picking up something really different, working on another hobby etc.. If I do, my 'idle' state of training and running is something like Block 1 of the 9-mile marathon training schedule. Moderate length runs at MHR (2/week), an occasional interval/speed run with friends, fun-trail run, cross training, swim, bike, fitness whatever comes. 3 times per week basic 10-15 minutes core strength training is something you always keep doing.

If you're a true running lover (and I know MANY of you are!), another way of looking at the 3 months 'idle' time is to focus on another race distance like 10k or a half marathon. Or even a 5k race. Or, what I often do too, is to focus on an Ironman 70.3 or an Olympic distance Ironman. When you shift your focus from running and training for 26 miles to shorter distance races your mind and body are 'loosening up'.

To Many Of My Running Students, This Works Great

Your mind and body receive different stimuli, different impulses, allowing your body to develop one step further up.

9miler4life.com

Other things you could do between races: improve your strength with dedicated strength training in the gym, work on your technique, improve your hill climbing strength, signup for a training class on food, nutrition, trigger point therapy, etc. etc.

Let's talk about training for a 10k in the period of 2 months after your last marathon, before you start your next 90-day 9-mile marathon training program again. If you decide to do that, it would be a great beneficial impulse if you had shift your training to two interval trainings per week and one 2–5 mile run at your anticipated 10k race-pace (with a 2-3 mile easy warmup and a one mile cool down). Your heart rate would be at like 6-12 bpm higher than the MHR you used at your 9-mile marathon training. So your heart rate for your 10k training AND race would be like MHR + 6 to 12.

Find Out Which One Works Best For You

For some of you training at MHR + 6 bpm will already feel quite intense. While others 'digest' this training at MHR +10 bpm easily. It's very personal. Just go out there and test yourself.

On top of this 'intense' 10k training you would add a

Bi-weekly MHR run of 5-7 miles

to maintain your endurance.

Training like this would definitely improve your 10k pb. And it's fun! Plus it will DEFINITELY improve your next marathon performance!! Improving your 10k time is 100% related to improving your marathon finish time. You can look it up for yourself in the Finish Time Prediction Table.

When you do the CHR test AFTER you trained to improve your 10k time you will notice your CHR will have improved too. It is almost certain that your CHR will be heartbeats HIGHER than the last time you did the test. In most cases this will be in the range of 2 - 10 heartbeats higher. If you will pick up your marathon training AFTER you trained to improve your 10k time it is therefore required to re-calculate your MHR again based on your latest CHR test.

Oh and by the way. Time between races is the IDEAL time to talk and share about your 9-mile experiences with your friends. To share your stories at the 9-mile marathon 'closed' Facebook group.

Because You're Not Alone!

If you have specific objectives and targets you could consider my 9-mile marathon one-on-one coaching program for a next 90 day period. In the one-on-one coaching program I will support and guide you 24/7 with your next level goals. Check www.9miler4life.com for more information!

19. THE #1 MISCONCEPTION

"You simply can't run a full marathon with only a couple of 9-mile training runs.."

..because you MUST run more miles in order to:

1. 'Harden' yourself self through running at least a couple of 18+ mile long and slow training runs.
2. Only when you ran like 20 or 22 miles you know you're ready for the full distance.

This is what I hear most. A BIG misconception!

Based On Assumptions

The 9-Mile Marathon training system is a carefully balanced, comprehensive concept, based on more than just running less miles. Finding your MHR, your marathon heart rate sweet spot, is essential. You will be running ALL your 6-9 mile training runs AND your marathon at this particular heart rate MHR.

In the 'regular' marathon training plans you run your long training runs SLOWER and at LOWER hr.

If You Think About It, It Doesn't Make Sense.

I found this EXTREMELY ineffective.

The 9-Mile training system is based on AFA (the concept of Accumulated Fatigue Avoidance) and ESS (initiating the metabolic Energy Supply Switch). On top of that, there is the importance of Cross training, getting rid of the rigid (both physical and mental 'loose' approach to the schedule) and 9-mile specific speed- and interval training (full recovery type of interval sets).

In the regular' training plans there is no emphasize on cross training and strength/core training. Dead wrong in my opinion.

The 9-Mile Marathon Training Program is a cleverly balanced thoroughly thought-through concept, very effective, highly efficient.

From ALL successful 9-Mile Marathon runners I have trained in the past I can assure you his:

The ANSWER to both 1. ('HARDEN' yourself) and 2. (to 'KNOW' you can do it) is a BIG

"No, Not True."

You DO NOT need to harden yourself through running those endless long and slow training runs. The 6 to 9-mile training runs are at your marathon heart rate and therefore at marathon pace. It appears they 'harden' you well enough to get you ready for the big day. With less risk on injury and mental exhaustion. GIVEN your busy life with work, family and friends.

The 9-Mile Marathon concept represents a new APPROACH to 'balancing' training effectiveness, efficiency and fatigue accumulation. With a MUCH greater emphasize on AVOIDING fatigue accumulation while STRENGTHENING yourself effectively to prepare your body for the big day. You have to realize you only need to run 26 miles ONCE! With the classic programs you push your physique in such a way you almost do the full distance every week. Why? This is only wearing you out. Definitively.

'TRADITIONAL' training programs are STOPPING you from RELEASING the full POWER within you when it is needed most: on RACE DAY!

It seems for MOST age-goup runners in the range of 3 to 6 hours finish times, those repetitive long runs are counter-productive.

They Do More Harm Than Good.

That's why most of my students run the marathon STRONGER the 9-miler way! It is the proof to me that those constant 6-9-mile training runs (twice per week) make your body stronger and even better prepared than running 18+mile slow runs.

The mental challenge to run your marathon with only 6-9mile training based program appears ONLY ONCE; at your first marathon 'The 9-Miler Way'. Yes, you have to trust the system. What helps is that you will start to feel stronger and stronger all the way. A HUGE BOOST in self confidence BY FOLLOWING THE 9-MILE MARATHON WAY of training. Because training at your MHR will make you faster AT your MHR week-after-week.

Now That's A Big Confidence Boost!

Once you have experienced the benefits you will have the answers by experience. You will feel

INCREDIBLY strong at the starting line. By running 6-9 mile training runs at MHR (your calculated personal marathon heart rate sweet-spot) and the smart 9-Mile training schedule, you will prepare yourself

'Just Good Enough',

without ANY trace of fatigue accumulation.

This proves to be the BIG SECRET of The 9-Mile Marathon training system. Independent of the way we train, we'll all feel tired around 20-24 miles. Those 'traditional' 18 mile long training runs aren't preparing you for this either! It is my personal experience that training The 9-Miler Way is a MUCH BETTER WAY to survive those last miles, and to recover quicker after the race. With another HUGE benefit: less stress on your social life and your physique during the months of preparation. Meaning there will be energy left for friends and family during the weekends.

20. EPILOGUE

My entire running career I trained the classic way. No options, no alternatives. This was the only way to go. The whole running community agreed. We didn't know any better. Long runs, moments/periods of total exhaustion, recovery during your prep weeks, taper periods, getting colds, trying to manage your daily schedule with your work, business, family, kids, husband, always on the edge. Training was only good when times were faster than the last time. Training was only good when you felt completely wasted. No pain no gain.

Today We Have A Choice

The 9-Mile Marathon is a serious alternative to the classic way of endurance training. Yes, it is COMPLETELY DIFFERENT from the classic way of training. It requires a different mind set. Running long while training for a marathon is not a status thing anymore. Bribing about the number of miles you ran during the weekend either.

The 9-Mile Marathon is a game changer. 9-Milers are the rebels of the running society. They MAKE the new rules. "I only ran 8-9 mile training runs and I finish my best marathon ever". A new mantra.

I truly believe that to most marathon runners-- who live a normal busy life with work, family and friends-- this new approach has HUGE VALUE to offer.

The 9-Mile Marathon allows you to prepare and run a marathon as an integrated part of your life, without dominating it.

Not everybody is enthusiastic about The 9-Mile Marathon training program, the concept and the disruptive thinking. To say the least. A large group of trainers call the method crazy. A hoax. Fake news. Even though there are many great examples now of runners successfully adopting my new 9-mile schedules, many classic trainers keep on claiming 9 mile training runs are absolutely insufficient to prepare yourself for the full distance.

In their opinion suffer and exhaustion is part of the marathon game. They say pain is part of the beauty of marathon running.

I have lived and tried both worlds. And I, too, became very enthusiastic about this new training paradigm in probably the most difficult time of my life in 2014 (read Chapter 1). Although I am at the edge of the spectrum with my fastest marathon time of 2h47, I can still see the benefits of this disruptive approach, in particular for the 'average' age-group runner. In fact, it brought me the World Championship Ironman 70.3 and following happy years of high level sub 3 hours marathon running. The Dutch examples and stories of runners who adopted this philosophy, and the runners from our own training groups who did the same, are the proof for me.

9miler4life.com

I only shared in these pages those things that have been proven to work for me and many other runners. You can have faith, knowing that The 9-Mile Marathon program has been proven by hundreds of different runners.

To me, personally, The 9-Mile Marathon has many benefits. As a busy mom and as a business owner my life and happiness are completely linked to the amount of time in which I can manage to get things done, stay fit, stay focused when my family and friends need me to be there with them, get enough sleep, and keep my energy levels high.

The 9-Mile Marathon makes it easier for me to run marathons and Ironmans as integrated part of my life. I know many of you out there would love to run a marathon but simply cannot commit to 4 months of training with weekly 18+ miles long runs and running totals of 30 miles per week and more.

If you truly love to run the long runs, then The 9-Mile Marathon is not for you. When you are someone who likes to go out and run for hours, when running the long runs a couple of times per week is what makes you happy, then better stick with the 'old' way of training. But, to me, personally, it is clear now. Finally there is a new approach to training, running and finishing the marathon in a way that fits into your daily life. Better than the training schedules of the old days. With the same, or even better outcome. Which is to enjoy the journey, enjoy the event and to finish your race in the projected time, happy and healthy.

So for me, personally, the choice is made. I have become a convinced 9-Miler. And a passionate 9-Mile Marathon coach.

There is no way back. I'm a 9-Miler. Part of the new breed of marathon runners. And I love it.

21. FAQ

Why do you call it The 9-Miler way?

Running max 9-mile training runs is the cornerstone of the training program. But there is more. Much more. The 9-Mile Marathon is a carefully balanced, comprehensive SYSTEM, based on more than just running less miles. Finding your MHR, your marathon heart rate sweet spot is essential. We do that with a test protocol -explained in the program- you can do yourself (with an explanatory video). AFA (the concept of Accumulated Fatigue Avoidance) and ESS (initiating the metabolic Energy Supply Switch) are dominant factors as well. Furthermore there is the importance of Cross training, getting rid of the rigid (both physical and mental) and 9-mile specific speed- and interval training (full recovery type of interval sets). All 'n all a cleverly balanced thoroughly thought-through concept, very effective, highly efficient.

Does it mean that what I've been doing in the past is a waste (effort)?

No! By no means no! My goal is not to FIX what's not working for you. My goal is to REPLACE what's not working with something NEW. Based on whatever you did in the past. Most people have TRIED to improve in the past, and for some reason it didn't work. They've tried to lose weight. They've tried to improve their running. Now it's time to move FORWARD. I'm offering a possibility to start training a NEW way.

And what if I LOVE running and training those long runs?

Well, if you LOVE running long, and you feel happy and healthy with it, please KEEP DOING IT! I am not saying The 9-Mile Marathon training system is for everybody. If you've been STRUGGLING with your marathon running, or if progress is staying away, I advise you to switch from the traditional 'no pain no gain' training to The 9-Miler way.

Is this a good program for my first HALF marathon?

Oh yes indeed! The 9-Mile Marathon training program contains a HALF marathon specific program as well. We have only one go-no-go though. We want you to be able to run a 10k in less than 75 minutes. This applies to both half- and full marathon. When you need more than 75 minutes to finish your 10k we advise you to improve your 10k running first. Because it would take more than 6 hours to finish which -I believe- is not a healthy thing anymore. In the 9-Mile Marathon Training program you will find Interval and Speed training exercises to make you faster.

My best 10k is more than 75 minutes and/or my best 5k is like 35 minutes. Any advise?

We want you to be able to run a 10k in less than 75 minutes. This is the requirement for both half- and full marathon. When you need more than 75 minutes to finish your 10k we advise you to improve your 10k/5k running first. In the 9-Mile Marathon Training program you will find Interval and Speed training exercises to make you faster. That will be a better start. When you run 75minutes or more on the 10k, it means you will need more than 6 hours on the marathon. Which I personally think can't be considered as true marathon running anymore. While The 9-Mile Marathon is made for marathon <u>runners</u>.

Can I switch to The 9-Mile Marathon schedule from another program?

As long as there are 90 days left, YES, you can! With less than 90 days your body will not have time enough to fully adapt to the specifics of The 9-Mile Marathon training program. There are hundreds of athletes who used the 9-mile program now. The closer they stick to the plan, the bigger chance they finish their marathon strong.

I want to run my best marathon possible. Is The 9-Mile Marathon system the way to go?

Yes. I have developed The 9-Mile Marathon training system to allow YOU to run your best marathon at THIS particular moment in THIS particular situation. So I am looking at 'performance' from a different angle. When you have a busy job, running a family and living a social life, you will

NEVER be able to run your fastest marathon at the same time (in absolute sense). With The 9-Mile Marathon training program you will run your best marathon GIVEN your personal circumstances.

To some, The 9-Mile Marathon will be the best training method available on the market today to run your fastest marathon ever. I have students in my running group who ran marathons in the past and ran pb's from the moment they started to work with The 9-Mile Marathon.

I want to do ultra running this winter, like 35 mile trail runs. Is the 9-Mile Marathon training system applicable?

Yes. Absolutely. In fact the 9-Mile Marathon training system is DERIVED from ultra running concepts. And, even more specific, from medical rehab strategies to help patients recover from setbacks as fast and effective as possible. It appeared that at specific heart rates, moderate length/endurance, balanced repetition and differentiation the healing/recovery process can be accelerated substantially.

9miler4life.com

I am a triathlete. Can I use the 9-mile program to train for the run part of triathlon?

Again yes. Absolutely. That's what I've been doing the past Ironman seasons. Which led to becoming world champion Ironman 70.3 in my age-group. The only thing I add to running the 9-miler way is combining it with the bike part. So, the so called 'brick' trainings (first bike than run) I do "The 9-Miler Way!"

I am planning to run 2 full marathons in one month. How can I use The 9-Miler way of training?

Interesting question. The answer is yes you can, and use the "Block 1" training intensity in between your races (as I have explained in the training program). Your challenge will be to not hurt yourself. Injury will come due to training overload. So you have to DRASTICALLY decrease your training workload. The intensity of "Block 1" of The 9-Mile Marathon training system may do the job for you.

YOUR NEXT STEP IS TO EXECUTE

9MILER4LIFE

YOUR GUIDE TO RUNNING THE 9-MILER WAY

WITH:

EVERYTHING YOU NEED TO MAKE IT *HAPPEN*: TABLES, SCHEDULES, HELP, TIPS, FORMULAS, DAY-TO-DAY PROGRAMS, CORE STRENGTH TRAINING EXERCISES, RUNNING EFFICIENCY, BREATHING SECRETS, WORKBOOK,

DAY-TO-DAY COACHING PROGRAM
24/7 ONE-ON-ONE SUPPORT

AUDIO BOOK
..AND MORE

GO TO **9MILER4LIFE.COM**

Notes:

You Don't Have To Play This Game Alone.

There are marathon runners, including me, who want to welcome you as a 9-Miler and support you on your Marathon Running journey.

Will You Join Us?

The Choice Is Yours:
www.9miler4life.com

Made in the USA
San Bernardino, CA
05 December 2018